A Common I

Shashi

Table of Contents

Dedication

My book is for everyone who touched my life in a way that
made it better.

About The Author

Shashi is a businessman who went from living from hand to mouth to owning a multi-million-pound business. Shashi was born in a small town, Kaliari, in India, to a poor farmer and his wife. For most of his early life, his father struggled to make both ends meet through farming.

However, life went on until one day, Shashi found his father's lifeless body on the floor one day. From that point on, he started experiencing life at its ugliest. It was only after his eldest brother sponsored his mother and him to the UK that Shashi saw hope ahead in life.

In the UK, Shashi had a tough choice between education and business. He picked the latter and started off with a convenience store. Meanwhile, he got married to a wonderful woman named Mina, who supported him at all times, and the couple was blessed with three smart and beautiful daughters.

Shashi's life changing decision was to start a coffee franchise, which made him wealthy with time. He worked hard to upgrade his business and ended up owning a coffee brand some decades later. After experiencing a brutal heart attack, he bid farewell to the business in favour of a healthy life. Now, Shashi spends his time with his growing family and together, Mina and he raise their grandchildren in the best possible way

Chapter 1: The Beginning

If I calculate back manually, it was around 1917 that my father was born, and my Mother was born in 1923. We don't have their exact date of birth since in those days record-keeping was not the most important of things; or as the Westerners would call it, "you were not smart enough to keep records."

My parents were united by an arranged marriage ensured by my grandfather. I assume they met each other at my father's or mother's home, and both agreed to the marriage, and so it came about. Back in those days I tell you, marriage was a ritual. There was not much hoo-ha about it, it was an obligation that had to happen since a man needed a wife to do housework, and a woman needed a husband for financial support. That was the traditional set-up in our indigenous Indian culture.

My parents did not give birth to children for a very long time, but eventually we did come about. So, my eldest brother was born in 1955 when Jawaharlal Nehru was still the Prime Minister of the country. Since my brother was the first child of our family, he was naturally the spoilt and pampered one. I mean, as pampered and as spoiled as he could be on an annual income that was no more than 30,000 rupees. That would be 300 pounds in today's amount. So it is very convenient to say, our financial position was well below the poverty line.

Not just my parents but even my ancestors were farmers; farming is all our family knew. You cannot say that all farmers live below the poverty line. Much depends on the land and other factors, all the thin

gs we were not very fortunate in.

Naturally as it goes, land had been diminishing across generations in our family. The way land system works in farming is, suppose you have 100 acres of land for a child. If you have another child, that hundred acres of land will be divided 50 acres each between the two children. Then 25 acres each for four children, and so on. And this distribution or partition of land was based across a whole household. My father had three other brothers. On the opposite side, my other uncle had one son. So, one part of the land was dedicated to one person, that is my one cousin off that uncle, and my father's part of land was divided among four people. We collectively owned 25 acres of land.

Because the water situation was terrible in the farms, the farmers in our family had to rely on the monsoon season, where heavy rainfall is expected. Back in 1960, monsoon season lasted 4 months a year. My family would get rice crops in the monsoon, then would have to wait for summer to grow mangoes. And the trend in our farm was that if you get one good harvest of crops, the other one always let you down. Or vice versa. You could do nothing about it, it was as if decreed by God himself.

When my second brother was born, everything remained the same, except now there was an extra person to feed. To give you some details about our house, we did not have any television or any entertainment system at our place. Most we had was my uncle who had an old radio. It was from there that they would get to hear the daily news. There was no other medium to get any outside knowledge in. My family barely managed their day to day living in 1961, so we surely did not have the mind to concern ourselves with politics and current affairs. It was a self-enclosed kind of a life. My eldest brother went to live with my uncle. It was from his house that he would to go to school from. My middle brother was going to school from home by 20th April 1963.

It was in this environment that I stepped into this world. I was number 11th and final child among all my cousins between four uncles. The land therefore had been shared up till my generation. So my father had ended up with 25 acres of land, and my portion was barely 8 acres.

As I started growing up, I noticed the hardship of my parent's life. They were barely living a hand-to-mouth life. Fulfilling desires was not how it worked in my family. I used to wear both of my elder brothers' old clothes and shoes. It was not that my parent were lazy, no sir! They were trying their hardest to give us everything within their means. But you can barely do anything at 30k a year income. So we lived a very simple life dotted with day to day struggle. The smell of the soil and visions of vegetation come to mind thinking of my childhood days.

Despite all of this, we never complained. My mother had made it clear that if we can't afford it we can't have it. This lesson alone had taught us a lifelong lesson to live within our mean. The struggle continued for future years. We became a part of it, and struggle became a part of it. It hurt when we would see other kids wearing new clothes on Diwali festivals and we couldn't afford it. Given our limited knowledge and thinking, we did not even know how we were going to get out of this situation, if we ever were. Below you can find some pictures of the house we had back then, and both my parents.

My wife was from another village. When I got married to her, I did not get any land in dowry. This was unusual since this was not the case usually. My wife also came from a background of farmers. The reason why we didn't get any land was that this time, the dowry ritual was over. We had stopped believing in dowry, and had stopped imposing it. In some ways, that was a good thing to inherit, since dowry is a major cultural issue we face in South Asia.

My parents had coached all us brothers hard in the values of discipline and principles. Hard work was essential in our family, and it is from there that I also inherited my discipline from. Up until this time, my work ethic and discipline in life has been paved way for great success. I owe my discipline and fortitude that my parents distilled in me for that. Their way of passing on values was so great that despite being a middle aged man, all the lessons my family taught me are ingrained within me sharply and vividly. Whenever I think about my parents at this age, I imagine them sitting before me and giving advice about life, experiences and, of course about expenses. That was always a humbling process. Even though they did not have much time, they would make it a point to portion out some time for their children. These gatherings were their way of making us understand what was happening in the family and how they were handling the budget.

Come to think of it, I have instilled the same set of values to my offspring. I have coached them in hard work and discipline, and it has yielded me great results. I do also believe that I have gone further too, which I shall get to in a bit.

My eldest daughter was born in 1986, only six years after I came to England. You might be thinking, if I was not well-off, why did I decide to leave India in the first place? You will get to see that it was not by choice that I went abroad. My brother took advantage of the situation and as soon as he turned 18, he went abroad and later sponsored my mother, and little old me tagged along. We'll get to all that later on.

But by that time when I had my first daughter, I was still living the life of a poor man. I was starting to earn money, and little by little, was starting to get things off the ground. I decided to enrol my daughter in a private school as soon as she got of age. Turns out, my priority with each of my three daughters was to get them a top-notch education. For me, it did not matter as much whether they could cook or not. I did not exactly hold that traditional line of thought. Cooking, cleaning and all the other household chores you can learn at any point in your life, truly. But there are deadlines and specific timings for primary, secondary and college-level education. Those timings have to be met, that too with dedication and devotion. There was never going to be a compromise on that on my part. I would prefer my daughter becoming a university queen rather than kitchen queen.

See, the thing I learned is that, once you have good education, especially a good degree, you will always have other things lined up and working well for you, especially in a western country. A degree mattered a lot to this world, and therefore, to me. It was the ticket to a good, prosperous life through a successful job. That was what I instilled in my daughters. And this was a trend that differed from the customs and traditions of my ancestors, family and parents.

You may be wondering what my wife would have made of my inclination towards studies over housework. I had told her in the beginning, right after I had two of my three daughters that "Do not teach anything in the kitchen to my daughters. Let them get a degree. If they want to learn something, they can learn after, since they are not going to run out of time to learn of culinary and kitchen discipline." My wife said, "Fine," and would sometimes joke with me. She would say, "Oh, you told me not to teach our daughters the kitchen work, and see now they can't even make an egg." I would always counter with saying, "No worries, there's still lot of time to learn all that." What mattered was their education was going well, and that was what would make me proud.

My philosophy in life is that if you have enough money, everything out there is for sale. If my daughters would have a good salary, they could hire any culinary expert later on to teach them whatever kitchen skills they desired. I don't know about you, but that to me makes great sense. The value of education is not simply for capitalistic, monetary purposes either. I laid emphasis on education also because of the social experience and how much an exposure to a healthy school and college life chisels one's personality. I wanted all of that for my daughters which I was deprived of.

My upbringing, of being a village boy under the mentorship of two farmer parents, compared to my daughters' upbringing was very different. I learned things firsthand from life, events, experiences. Everything was a phase for me, and I moved on, no matter how terrible times I had seen. I was still in my teens when I came into this country, when I learned that a comfortable life and success in a western world would have to come through adopting certain western values and paradigms. I preserved my Indian-ness, don't get me wrong. But I just caught on some different colours for the purpose of adaptation.

All the values that I had learned, I passed to my daughters as well. I let them know every chance I got that "I was not raised lavishly, was not brought up in a rich lifestyle, and so I learned all that I'm teaching you the hard way. Now we have money, we can buy anything we want, but we will not let that blind us. You have to make sure that you make something of yourself, and not be a failure."

Poverty was a constant state when I was growing up, we were almost never well-off. My daughters saw none of that, so they had to be told. We relied on borrowing from our relatives with the hope of paying them back. Whenever we would get surplus from our crops, we would little by little return to those we owed. If my daughters would not know about this, they would grow complacent and perhaps even prideful.

My childhood was riddled with struggle. I never got to see any toys. The only thing I could get to play with was making things out of mud, which would dry in the summer sun. We also played the local indigenous game of *gilli danda* where two teams are formed and they take turns to bat. The batsman tries to hit the *gilli* with the *danda* twice – once to lift it off the ground and once to hit it as far as possible. If he is successful in the hit, the fielding team tries to catch the *gilli* before it touches the ground. We would run hard and play all these games, all us siblings and cousins. These were our only leisure activities. When we'd find nothing else, we'd play with stones and marbles. Life was below the poverty line, and that was our way of having fun.

In retrospect, it is this very lifestyle of modesty, hardships, trials and difficulties that has made me the man I am today. It was far from a perfectly-planned life. The things that lacked in my life were what gave me the courage and energy to do something big. I'd have gone insane if I hadn't done anything. I had decided that I didn't want to carry on living a miserable life. As I will explain later on in the book, it was the second half of my life, when my father passed away and when I came to England that my life hit the rock bottom. That was when I ended up doing incredible things. I got many lessons on what you have to do if you want to be a successful person from that phase in life. None of that would have been possible though if not for my initial upbringing.

My parents were wonderful people. I would not have wished for a better pair of them. My mother came to England with me in 1980, and stayed till 1999 when she passed away. My mother has not only made me the man I am today but also looked after and helped raise my daughters well too. She had a role in humbling them as well.

I remember she would sit and recall how tough times were back in the day, what we went through, and how everything we had by now came through with toil and hard work. My girls always loved listening to those stories, they would be immersed in them. Sometimes they would ask their grandma, tell us something about our father's upbringing or our grandpa. My mother would relay all the stories about our way of life and what a great man my father was. And I would be left thinking that when I was young, my mother barely had time to talk to her children since her everyday life was so busy and full of chores. I was grateful that my daughters could get this level of supervision and blessing. Up until this day, my daughters acknowledge how inspired they were by my mother, and they miss her.

This makes me take pride in my daughters, my mother, and my own life.

Chapter 2: Kaliari

I was born in a small village called Kaliari to a pair of beautiful people. My parents were amazing people; they had small pockets with very big hearts. Since I was their final offspring, they were ecstatic at my birth. I was showered with all the love and attention. My parents kept me close to themselves so much that they even refused to send me to my uncle's house as part of the tradition.

Located in Navsari district in the state of Gujrat, my village Kaliari spans across a meagre 4.97 square kilometre. It is so tiny and insignificant that if you type it on google, you will get very little information about it. No doubt it was never very famous and not many outsiders visited it.

As much as I hold this place in high regard for giving birth to my parents and me and raising us, I cannot turn my head from the various ailments and lack of opportunities that plagued our lives there. It did provide us with basic sustenance in the form of land, for example, but that kept depleting with time, and there was no other way to make a decent living for ourselves.

Most people in the village had a very traditional mindset. For centuries, the inhabitants of this place had remained stuck in terms of progress, be it in economic terms or on the socio-cultural front. It was as if we were kept in prison without any contact with the world outside. Our concept of time and space had paused.

Perhaps if somebody had taken pictures of the people of this land centuries back and compared them with the current times, we could hardly spot any differences. With the same way of living, the same codes of conduct, the same poverty, the same problems, we had hardly progressed through the course of time.

It was not just our physical conditions that had remained constant, but our internal outlook too was as constant as a rock erected in a ditch the size of its body. Most people had backward beliefs and values. One could not muster the courage to move out of this rigid system because no one knew the path leading outward. This village meant the entire world to us. We knew little to nothing about the world outside because there was no way we could. We did not have a TV or any other means of communication with other parts of India.

Because of ignorance and illiteracy, the people of our village, including myself and my family, had a very narrow view of life. We would never set high goals or try to achieve something big; our benchmarks for all matters of life and success were way too low. We had no clue as to what big meant or even what goal meant, for that matter. Since we were surrounded by like-minded and equally ignorant people like ourselves, there was no possibility of growth or progress.

Unfortunately, multiple outdated norms and values became prevalent in our part of Gujarat. Particularly about gender discrimination, our society was very rigid. They would ordain the women to look after home chores. Their education was often compromised. They were married off against their will. Widows were treated poorly. Those beliefs would pass on to other generations, who lacked the mental capacity to differentiate good from the bad.

I don't blame my people for harbouring outdated beliefs and values. They would practice what they knew, and they knew little. They wanted to transfer our traditions to the next generation as they were, and I don't hold them accountable for that. They were not evil. It was just that their circumstances refused to allow their mind enough nourishment. Had they received better education and respectable earning opportunities, I knew for a fact they would fare better in social indicators.

What we call freedom of expression today was dormant in those times and ages. Forget about mammoth political or economic matters or debates surrounding human rights; we did not have the permission to decide on matters pertaining to our personal lives.

If you want to get a fair idea of the status of freedom, consider this. We were just not allowed to make a move to another place or marry the person of our choice. Everything about us would be decided by the elders. They could be right; they could be wrong. Whatever the case may be, it was the individual who suffered at the end of the day.

Nobody had the audacity to challenge the decisions of elders. Anybody who tried to be an outcast would face extreme sort of rejection and ostracism. Since our small village meant the world to us, we could not dare to face such dire consequences of rebellion. Therefore, we chose the safest option of compliance.

People boast about things from their village; I hardly had anything exciting to talk about or yearn for. Some miss food; others miss recreation; yet others feel nostalgic about the moments of peace and solitude they enjoyed with the village life. I cannot possibly miss the food because we hardly got enough—that which we got comprised of the bare minimum required to survive. I cannot bring myself to miss any well-known spots or significant sites because of a sheer absence of them from our village.

As far as recreation or entertainment went, we had very few opportunities. At most, we would play with marbles, or showcase our sports skills in *gilli danda*, or make objects with mud. that was the pinnacle of our recreation, and as we grew up, financial crises took my childhood away, and I had to make efforts to make both ends meet. I really wish I had enough good memories of my hometown like other people, but I had close to none. The only things I can recall when I close my eyes are troubles, ailments, and crises.

In the vast territory of India, my village hardly occupies a noticeable space. Despite Gujarat being touted as one of the best performing states in economic and social indicators, there are places whose backwardness knows no bounds. There were hardly any construction or development projects taken up in these areas. Most people, therefore, led a miserable life.

The rest of the Indians don't see any traction in our villages. If I talk about my particular village, I don't remember any famous buildings or sites where anybody would throng to. All around it was vast patches of land dotted with grazing livestock. There were barely any proper roads connecting us to the other parts of India.

My two elder brothers used to live with our uncle as per the tradition. Their residence was in a less backward village than ours, about 50 kilometres away. It was an ordeal to get to their village and meet them. We had to take a public bus from far off station and jolt along our way. Mind you, the fare was a big chunk of our income, and therefore, we had to think several times before undertaking any such journey.

Such was the level of underdevelopment that there was no place of worship, *mandir*, in the entire village. My mother would get the pictures of our gods and put them around our small house to seek their blessings. We would hang them up on the walls to keep them away from dirt and filth. Also, since we would sleep on the congested floor, we had to make sure our feet don't touch the pictures of our gods. There was no better place than the walls of our house for them.

People of my village would spend most of their time in the fields. The only means of income for us was harvesting. If you wanted to see the class difference in my village, the biggest manifestation of it would be the amount of land they own. There were large landowners, on the one hand. They had huge agricultural areas in their name. There, they could grow more crops that would translate into greater profits at the time of harvest.

Most of the time, these landowners had sizeable livestock. They might not be super rich by modern standards, but they made abundant cash, ample food, and other products such as dairy and meat from the livestock. However the circumstances turned out, they rested assured that they wouldn't starve to death. Their children went to bed with a full stomach, and they enjoyed a reasonably lavish lifestyle. By lavish, I mean they ate three meals a day, wore new clothes, had better homes with sufficient articles of daily use.

On the other end of the spectrum were the low landowners, such as ourselves. We could only grow two crops on our land. That, too, was a laborious task, replete with risks. We would work in scorching sunlight and through light and dark. Not just that, we also had to take the necessary measures to protect the crop as it was the only source of income for our big family. Once the crop was sown, we would guard it day and night. After all these efforts, we would get the result in no less than six months.

We did not have the luxury of growing more than two crops. The big landowners, on the other hand, had this option. They would grow crops over a larger area and thereby get greater produce. Some could grow multiple crops on their land. These people certainly made a lot more money than us. Hence, we had absolutely no way by which we could escape this vicious circle of poverty we were born into.

If we were lucky, we would receive what we had sown. In the other scenario, our crops would be attacked by pests or some environmental hazard, and we were left mourning over the losses. I am not a huge fan of crying over spilt milk, but what else could a prisoner of time do? Could he escape to some unfound land? Or could he make a decent living for himself when he did not know any skill other than farming? Or could he turn the wheel of time backwards and fix everything from the beginning? Indeed, he could not do any of these.

Growing up in a poverty-stricken household, seeing my parents fretting over the prospects of putting the next meal on the table was one of the most bitter memories I have. Our sleeping places were not far apart in our small home, which allowed me to overhear most of those painful midnight conversations my parents had about depleting finances and the list of uncertainties tomorrow could bring.

Despite being the youngest in my family, I grew up really fast. My brothers had left for the uncle's home way too early, and I was retained here by my loving parents, which equipped me with a lot of knowledge and exposure. I would work in the crops with my father. Everything that happened at work would be shared naturally with me. Since a very young age, I had known matters such as how much money we owed to who? How much do we have to survive on? What are the prospects of the next harvest to be abundant?

As a young kid, I would go to a public school, and that was all my parents could afford with their small income. I would never receive any pocket money as making both ends meet seemed an ordeal. I would gladly wear my school uniform and regular slippers and pick a few books in my hands before beginning the journey.

On the way, it would often start pouring, leaving the sand all wet and muddy. We would stride our way to the steps, taking careful steps to keep the mud off our feet. By the time we reached schools, our slippers had layers of caked mud underneath the sole. But since we were all in a similar state, there was no shame in exposing our spoiled belongings. On one of those days, I would miss having a pair of boots to protect my feet.

My school was always in a dilapidated condition since ever. The school walls could not protect us from the steaming heat or pouring rain. The roof of our classroom would leak heavily as though it could fall any minute. The ground was no heaven either. It would get all damp and cold, and we would spread some makeshift cotton rugs along to sit on, rather uncomfortably.

What could become of the students who were studying in such an environment? Were they given the state of the art teaching facilities? Of course not. But I had a little hope in my bosom that perhaps going to the school would enhance my exposure. Perhaps someday, I might be able to make a decent living out of what I have learnt at school. All of us students had similar hopes. Some were able to make it to that point where they could make something of their life, while the others stayed back in prison.

A very famous saying goes, *" 'when life throws you lemons, make lemonade"*. Perhaps I could not make lemonade out of my share of lemons, but I owe a lot of my achievements and successes to my circumstances. Today, when I recall my life events, I can clearly see how some of the apparently bitter experiences set the ground for making me a larger than life individual.

One of the best things poverty and deprivation have taught me is to value people and things. Thanks to my tough circumstances, I know the value of things, unlike those who were born with all the amenities of life. Growing up in my village, we would compromise our food so that the other person could fill their stomach. I am ever so grateful that now I have everything that was denied to me in my young years.

After spending most of my formative years with my father, I learned a lot of things way before time. I would closely watch my father interacting with his friends, neighbours, and other men while carrying out his routine activities. I would study people's words, behaviours, moods, and intentions. The exposure to work and people made me street smart. I was quick to learn the ways to deal with people and get my thing done.

Apart from that, all the problems I faced in life made me the person I am today. They enabled me to develop some highly valuable personal skills. Later events in life only polished them; the grounds were set in the very beginning. I cannot express my delight when people tell me I don't give up easily. If I have the ability to bounce back after setbacks, it is because of the myriad stumbling blocks that life put in my way without giving me the option to quit. I would jump higher and higher and practice hard to get better at jumping above the obstacles until I succeeded.

One of the most priced realization life made me absorb was that it was okay to fail, but remember to rise up and start afresh after every failure. If it weren't for my hardships, I would possibly never been this hardworking. Perhaps life was training me to become the best version of myself, and all the difficulties were my courses that school did not teach me.

Below are some pictures from my village:

Chapter 3: Childhood

Childhood is supposed to be one of the sweetest and carefree times of one's life. Generally, people define it as the time spent between the ages of 1 to 12 or 13. It is the phase in the life of an individual when their psychological development takes place because, during this age, they are absorbing the world around them and making sense of it. There is also active personality development taking place during this phase. The kind of environment a child is exposed to eventually shapes their perceptions and attitudes towards individuals and events.

Educated and enlightened people today are aware of the importance of this phase of life and therefore try to provide the best experiences to their children. Being a parent to three beautiful daughters myself, I am content that I tried to make my kids' childhood a memorable and productive one. People say childhood experiences are one of the most memorable ones, and rightly so. As I look back at my childhood, I can see flashbacks of the small me running around in the village with no slippers on and playfully walking on the way to school.

I spent all my childhood in Kaliari, unlike my brothers, who were there for a very short time. In total, I spent 14 long years there. During this time, I had experienced many moments of joy and sorrow. Perhaps everything that happened back then seemed joyful. A small child would only be cognizant of the present, immersed in more mundane, day to day tasks and taking out some time for play instead of planning about the future. Like every child of my age and background, my small mind could not make big decisions, and all I would do was busy myself with routine tasks of the day.

When I was small, my family and a few close friends meant the world to me. I would spend most of my time with either my mother or father or playing around with the friends I had made from the neighbourhood. My small eyes had seen them around since they began registering characters in their memory, and they could not imagine a world without them. Back then, I used to think I'd always be surrounded by these people, who were an essential part of my life.

In Kaliari, we had a very active morning routine. We would wake up at 5'o clock and get busy with our chores. They had already been divided among me, my father, and my mother. I, for instance, would freshen up and go to the buffaloes to milk them first thing in the morning. The milk then had to be taken to the dairy for sale. I will come back home and take a little bit of breakfast before getting ready for school.

My school timing was from 10'o clock in the morning to 5'o clock in the evening. All five days of the week, I would start from home early to reach the school in time and come back running from the school when the last bell rang. I actually looked forward to the pack up time because I had a number of tasks piled up. Apart from home, I would often manage to take some time out for having fun with my friends.

I remember rushing from school and putting my meagre belongings in the home before helping my mother with home chores. My mother would be needing me to do routine tasks, such as looking after the animals, giving them the food, cleaning the house, or bring her ingredients to be used in the meals. I would gladly run around and help my mother with her tasks.

Often times, I would help my father with work too. He would ask me to bring things to and from the farm, and I would merrily obey. At the farm, he would direct me to treat the crops a certain way, and I would follow him. He would do all the tasks very attentively, from sowing the seeds to watering the crop and ploughing the land with the help of buffaloes. He would examine the crops every now and then to ascertain they were secure from pests.

We would save chicken manure and cow dung to use as natural fertilizers for the crops. Those would be spread in the furrows to help the soil hold more nutrients and water, thereby getting more fertile. The more fertile the soil was, the better and abundant crops it produced.

After getting done with work, we would make sure no crows or animals attacked the crops. For this, we would erect scarecrows at small distances from one another, and the birds kept away. Despite that, we would have to check the crops every quite often to ascertain no animal had attacked them while we were away.

I acquired a great deal of knowledge regarding crops and farming just by watching my father go about his everyday tasks. I would watch him and offer my help in whatever piece of the task I could do. In my mind, I had acknowledged that sooner or later, I would be helping my father with farm chores and take after his duties to help him retire in peace. That was the future my small brain could imagine at that time, and perhaps it would turn out to be true had things remained the way they were.

Returning from the farm, we enjoyed our meal together. Meals, for us, were neither big nor sumptuous. For the most part, we had plain rice with lentils (*daal*). It was our staple. We would pour *daal* in the rice and mix the two evenly before taking a mouthful. Other times, we had small round *chapatis* with *daal* or some vegetable curry. Most of the food came from farm produce. We would save some for ourselves and sell the most.

For the most part of our life in Kaliari, we did not have the money to buy extravagant food items from the market. Therefore, we would survive on the little we had at home. Even that was not enough at times, and the three of us found ourselves sharing the food that would otherwise suffice for one person only.

On rare occasions, we would be invited to some function in the village. Somebody would hold worship prayers, *puja,* at their homes to get the blessings of gods. At other times, somebody would be celebrating the birth of a child. There would be weddings in the village too, with big men beating drums in a known rhythm and small children dancing to the beat. It was on one of these days that we treated our taste buds with delectable food and drinks.

When I was not directly involved in work, I was mostly looking after the animals. My father would often ask me to take the buffaloes to the riverside. I would pat the buffaloes on the neck and, in my own way, ask it to follow me to the river. It would come in scores and follow me along the way.

32

We'd have to traverse the vast fields and plain patches of land to finally get to the river.

At the river, I would sit on the rocks with my feet immersed in the water, panning my neck to keep an eye on the buffaloes while they sat in the river, enjoying the cold water splashes on its bodies. I would sometimes join in the fun and run water on their bodies. Other times, I would lie on the rock and stare at the clouds passing by. Some other times, I would watch other people and their animals bathing in water.

Where work was an integral part of our lives, fun was never ignored. I, in fact, looked forward to the time where my friends and I would gather and enjoy sports. We had some vast patches of dry land in Kaliari that served as playgrounds for us. We would mostly play *gilli danda* and cricket during the evening that would last until dusk.

Cricket was and still is to the major part a favourite sport of the Indians. It might sound strange, but people from some of the most primitive areas in India are well-acquainted with, rather are huge fans of, cricket. You could see children in barely any clothes on playing around with a bat and ball on the streets, in the grounds, and anywhere they find space just enough to host their game.

Not just that, the cricket craze is so high in India that you could go to faraway places and ask the children the names of their favourite cricketer. Most probably, they would have an answer to that despite having little to no access to mainstream media. Even without television and even electricity, people from our village would not miss those important cricket tournaments.

Sometimes, we would all gather at the house of that one person who had a TV. In fact, it would look like another stadium where people were sitting around the TV, peering at the screens in the cold nights with their shawls draped on the shoulders and covering the better part of their face. There would be old men squinting their eyes and watching the show with the utmost attention, and there would be small children dancing at every big shot hit or every wicket taken.

Our cricket mania was no small matter. We desperately wanted India to win every match it was a part of. There could be no bigger excitement than that of cricket lovers in the last few overs that would decide the fate of the match. As the match progressed, there would be little speculation and more silence until the final moment, when the crowd would burst into either cheer of victory or sorrowful deliberations on the match that would last for days to come until something else captured people's attention.

Cricket was also my favourite sport in childhood. We did not have any fancy bats or hard balls, but we would very well do without them. We would arrange a makeshift bat, often in dilapidated condition, and a tennis ball. That was all we needed to satiate our thirst for sports. We would be divided into teams and scattered all across the ground. Every one of us wanted to get a chance to showcase our skills at bowling, batting, fielding or all three of these.

We would also hold matches with the other team, and the winning team would get no trophy but a symbolic victory, which seemed like the ultimate goal for us. The man of the match could be spotted on the shoulders of the rest of the team, rising high among his friends, yelling and cheering for victory. Such was the extent of joy among the kids while playing cricket.

As a child, some of the fondest memories I have are from the religious festivals that came once a year and were celebrated with full zeal and devotion. Two of the main festivals were Holi and Diwali. It was when either of these was around the corner that we happened to get new clothes. However, there were some hard times when we could not, but at the end, we would wear an old pair of kurta and pyjama and submerge in the feel of the festival.

On Holi, we throw powdered colour on our fellows all day and compete in who colours who first. I would receive the first patch of colour from my parents, after which I'd go and meet my friends. I would fill both my hands with powdered colour and unleash them on my friends, instantly running away from them when they tried to do the same. We would laugh, run, and play all day until retiring to our beds, exhausted from intense activity.

On Diwali, we would burn firecrackers to celebrate the festivities at night. As for ourselves, we wouldn't get to buy them every time for Diwali. However, I loved seeing my friends cracking them and jumping at the bangs produced by each of them exploding in the air. I would often join them in fun and sometimes borrowed a couple to crack myself.

The best part of these festivals was the family time we got to spend together and the faint feelings of abundance they brought along. In my 14 years in Kaliari, there was not a single event that we celebrated in a grand way, but it was the little moments of happiness that filled our bosoms with a lot of happiness. These occasions brought some rare glimpses of delight, such as seeing my mother wearing a new *saari*, my father putting on a new pair of sandals, and us eating nice food after a long time. Those were the moments

I used to cherish from the bottom of my heart because they were scarce and did not happen every year.

The most integral part of all the occasions was prayers. We lacked a spacious mandir in our vicinity, but that did not keep us from praying. We would take the picture of the diety and decorate it with flower garlands before commencing prayers. Next, we would hold small prayer sessions at our homes, with my mother leading the two of us, who sat nodding our heads in a specific rhythm. My parents were very devoted followers of deities. Not just that, they were great human beings too, who followed the teachings of their gods in letter and spirit.

I never saw my parents committing any illegal or sinful act. Despite limited resources, my parents made sure they never cheated or fooled anybody. They preferred to eat less food and work extra hard than feeding their stomachs on ill-gotten money. My parents always chose the right and virtuous path and raised me to do the same. It was due to their upbringing that I always made my way up with sheer hard work and dedication and never used any sinful means to make more money.

There were also collective prayers that were being held at the house of some of the neighbours. We would all gather there and seek the blessings of our gods. The elders would hold *puja*, sometimes enjoyed small religious plays being performed in front of them, and the children would come up with their own ways of having fun in the gathering.

My friends and I would meet up and talk about the everyday affairs facing us. Just like myself, they, too, had a tiny worldview. Their lives, too, revolved around farming. Most of them had no plans other than carrying on agriculture and farming and helping their family make both ends meet. Sometimes, we would lay on the ground, tired of playing, and follow the stars with our gleaming eyes. Those were the times when we discussed our version of the world outside our world, Kaliari. Perhaps there was an urge to explore other lands in our tiny minds.

Chapter 4: Brothers

Being the youngest brother of three has both perks and challenges. I had the privilege of spending more time with my parents because I was the youngest of three brothers. My father kept me with himself. My parents arranged for my education in the public school within our village Kaliari. Apart from acquiring education, I would learn different trades by virtue of living with my parents. From a very early age, I had lived close to my parents and received most of their love and attention.

I was born into a family where the male child was sent to live over at their uncle's house. In my case, it was my maternal uncle's house where my two elder brothers were sent over. It was certainly not easy for my parents to send their precious than life kinds away. They, nonetheless, did that to ensure my brothers received better education and had better livelihood prospects.

My uncles' villages were a tad more advanced than our own. There, my brothers received a better education. They'd rub shoulders with slightly more knowledgeable people than ourselves. All this was done in the hope that this better environment would enable them to land a promising career.

When I was tiny and just started to make sense of the world, I remember there was a boy who came to our place quite rarely. My parents introduced him as my 'oldest brother'. I remember him being a kind and enlightened individual. He would wear shorts and buttoned shirts. His clothes were always neat and proper, not opulent of course, but good enough to make him look presentable. He slicked his hair backward with a comb and exuded an aura of self-assuredness and composure.

I have very few memories of him from my early childhood because he had gone to my uncle's place before I was even born. I only remember that he came to visit us at. He liked playing with me; he would often teach me lessons about life and things in general. He spoke in a gentle tone and had a tendency to provide elaborate explanations. He was kind was soft-spoken; it was a treat talking to him.

The name of my eldest brother was Bhikhu. Usually, he came to visit us twice a year. Due to school, he could not meet with us frequently. Hence, he would come first during the school summer vacations, which lasted for about six weeks. Then, he would come another time for about four weeks of Diwali holidays.

His arrival was a moment of absolute joy and celebration for us. We would be awaiting his arrival in advance. Once he came, we offered him the best of everything; my mother would cook his favourite food. We would save pure milk and yoghurt to use when he came around.

Even though he came for a short time, we actually bonded with each other very well. We played cricket together. Both of us were huge fans of cricket. We would discuss it with each other and develop opinions based on the discussions. At Diwali, he'd bring us sweets and firecrackers from his village, and we went running through the streets with a mouthful of sweets, bursting firecrackers, jumping and laughing along the way.

He was a gentleman from the heart. He had productive habits. He would not waste his time wandering around the streets or sitting idle; rather, he would study hard and made sure he completed the course well before time. Bhikhu brought a pile of books in his cloth bag even when he visited us. We'd find him reading all the time. He would be so absorbed in his books that he hardly could perceive what was happening in the surroundings.

I remember he was the one who made me want to study. I knew Bhikhu was going to become a big man someday. His habits and demeanour expressed he would be a successful individual eventually. He did become one. He is the most educated member of our family today. He earned his

Chartered accountant certification and has vast experience of working with notable firms under his belt.

I was extremely inspired by my brother because he knew much more than we did, and he always had a broad perspective on things. He was keenly interested in acquiring knowledge. It was pretty evident that he wanted to become an educated, career-oriented man in the future. I would listen closely when he spoke as if devouring each and every word coming out of his mouth. The time I spent with him was never wasted; there was just so much learning and grooming for me in it.

Bhikhu inspired me to aim high in life, acquire education and make good money. Those were the dreams of my entire family, but seeing Bhikhu working towards them so actively and diligently, I adopted the same subconsciously. If somebody had asked me back then who I wanted to grow up like, I would have, without a second thought, responded with, "Bhikhu".

Bhikhu had better finances than us since he was the oldest one and came from a slightly more developed place. He would buy new clothes and give the older ones to me. He'd purchase new slippers and give his older pair to me. I would wait for him to get new accessories so that I would get his used things. Those I would wear for the most part until he bought more and gave the previous ones to us.

Bhikhu had a caring nature. He would often inquire about us; he wanted to know if we were doing okay. Back at our home, he would busy himself helping my father and mother in whatever capacity he could. After my father's demise, when our financial condition got worse, we did not inform Bhikhu. But when he got to know, he regretted not being there and not being able to do something and later made up for it when he was in a position to do so.

Bhikhu had an influential personality. His knowledge and conduct resembled that of an educated person from a very young age. He was aware of how he was privileged to be able to attend a better school and had better prospects of earning good education. He was very ambitious himself. He wanted to acquire a respectable degree and make a decent earning out of it. We would be delighted to know that Bhikhu was working for his dream by performing well at studies.

Bhikhu instilled the desire for studies in me. He was the first to break this cycle of poverty and move to the UK. It was all thanks to him that I went there too. Perhaps if it weren't for him, I had stayed in Kaliari all my life. Bhikhu wanted to make sure we escaped poverty and came to the

UK. He sponsored my mother and me to enter the UK and hosted us at his place until I could stand on my own feet.

When I was small, my middle brother was there at our home. Hence, I have multiple memories of him from our childhood. We would run around and play games together. We were very fond of each other, and we had lots of fun together.

My middle brother's name was Jayanti. Jayanti was quite different from both of us. He was a silent boy; he spoke less and listened more. He wasn't as social as we were. He would spend time with us and involve in the activities we did but not as enthusiastically as us. He was rather reserved and, owing to his reserve nature, wouldn't bond with everybody easily.

He was sent away from us at a tender age to my uncle's village. He would study there, and we hoped he followed the footsteps of Bhikhu. Both Bhikhu and Jayanti were spared the trouble of farming since both lived away from us. They knew how it worked, but they were lucky not to do it every single day. My parents hoped this way they could focus on their studies and become educated men when they grow up.

By nature, Jayanti was kind. He was very soft-spoken and sensitive. He would get distraught if he learned of anything that was troubling my parents. He had a strong sense of responsibility towards the family. He loved and respected my parents; we meant the world to him. Our happiness would make him happy, and our tragedies would move him to tears.

Sensitive people are generally responsible individuals because they look after the needs of others well. They sense the troubles and ailments of those around them. They are mostly keen observers who perceive the feelings of others way quickly. The same was the case with my middle brother. He was so responsible that he gave up his education after my father passed away.

Jayanti took up farming to support the family. He had such a compromising soul that he did not think twice before taking the decision of quitting his studies. He was concerned about our future and my mother's growing age that he would do anything in his grip to provide us comfort.

Jayanti picked up farming to make both ends meet for us and stayed back in India till his death. He sacrificed not only his education but also gave up on his career prospects. While Bhikhu and I came to the UK, Jayanti spent all his life in Kaliari. He would work there and support his family. We'd talk on the phone and meet when I visited India. After a long time, when I went to meet him, he was the same Jayanti from the inside; that is, his heart was as pure as it was before. However, his health had started showing signs of concern.

Jayanti started looking old and ailing. He was fighting heart disease. After some time, he passed away from a heart attack. The news of his demise shattered us. I immediately went to India to perform the last rites of my compassionate brother. We bathed him, laid him in the wooden logs and cremated his body. That was our last meeting with Jayanti, who had made tall sacrifices for our family.

Despite living far from us, Jayanti had only goodwill and best wishes for our future. Whenever we met and told Jayanti about our progress in life or business, Jayanti's lips would stretch in an ear to ear smile. He had a warm smile. He was extremely happy for our prosperity. He only had prayers and positivity to send our way. Even though we lived pretty far away from one another, I think his prayers kept us protected from all evil and definitely contributed to our well-being.

Bhikhu, Jayanti, and I had lived separately for a major part of our lives, with only a few meetups in between. However, our bond stayed very strong. We had always loved one another and cared for each other even when we were away. We made multiple sacrifices for our collective benefit because we genuinely wanted only good for each other. In difficult times, we were always there to support our family in whatever way we could. We always prayed for each others' health and prosperity. Such was the bond among the three of us.

Here are the pictures of my brothers and me.

Chapter 5: School Days

My school life was very different from the routine life kids these days have. My daughters were privileged to go to a good school on private conveyance. They wore nice clothes to the school and had adequate accessories needed to function properly. They would have everything an ordinary child could wish for. It makes me feel immensely happy that my daughters had a wonderful academic experience; it was diametrically opposite to what I had experienced in my childhood.

As I look back and recall my school life, I cannot help drawing a contrast between where I started from and where I have reached in life. Where other people start from zero, my journey started much behind that mark. I lacked access to quality education and resources to afford one. I am absolutely elated that despite such a low beginning, I have achieved a lot in my life and was able to give my family everything I couldn't afford for myself.

I got admission into a government-owned school at the age of five. It was a small school in my village, Kaliari. A couple of friends of mine from the neighbourhood and I would go to school together. We did not have a fancy uniform. We wore shorts and a plain shirt. Most of the time, I would be wearing the old clothes of my eldest brother.

That, too, weren't many. Hence, I had to wear the same pair over and over again until they were no longer in a wearable condition.

Where children from affluent backgrounds went on vans and school buses, we walked our way to the school. The weather was not always kind on us. When it was hot, walking to the school and back home was an ordeal. When it rained, the sand would turn muddy, and we had to tread carefully along the way. Most of the times, I didn't have slippers on. By the time I reached the school, my feet would be all dirty. If that was not enough, I had to take up the muddy journey again on my way back home.

My school timings were from 8 in the morning to 5 in the evening. We started off much earlier to reach in time. I had minimal accessories for the school. We had a few books that served as the course books. I would hold them in my hand or use a cloth bag made by my mother to carry them in. Like clothes, I made judicious use of my brothers' books. I hardly had any proper stationery, except the bare minimum required to perform day to day activities, which included an ink bottle and a refillable pen.

One of the best things the school gave me was friends. They were from my neighbourhood as well, and we used to play and have fun together. We would desperately wait for recess time so that we could play our favourite games. We often shared exciting stories with one another during the break. That was all the fun we did.

Our school was in a very old building. It was quite old and hardly ever renovated. Nobody knew when the last time was the walls were painted. Whatever colour they were painted in had become some version of yellowish-white. My school had a basic infrastructure with a few rooms, one staff room, and a bathroom.

I don't remember seeing my school in good condition. There was hardly enough furniture to accommodate us. The walls were cracked, with paints peeling off everywhere. There wasn't any proper cleaning mechanism. You could sense a strange smell in the air because of uncleanliness and filth around that area. The washrooms were barely in usable condition. They stank so strongly with excreta overflowing that your nostrils would refuse to inhale the fetid air.

Our school didn't have elaborate subjects or courses. We had basic mathematics, science, and Hindi as part of our course. All our textbooks were in Hindi, which was the medium of instruction in the classroom as well. So, we were not exposed to English at school and therefore lacked the ability to communicate in it with others. I felt the disadvantage of not being exposed to English later in life.

During the monsoon, our school would be leaking all over. There would be water coming from the roof. The walls had become swollen by absorbing rainwater. They were getting weaker with each passing year. Our floor would get all wet, and we were made to sit on it and study for long hours. It was not a good experience sitting on the cold floor for an extended period of time, but we had no other choice.

Our teachers were simple people appointed by the government. In those days, it was not mandatory for teachers to have a certain minimum degree to be able to get a teaching job. Hence, most of my teachers were not highly educated. They had passed fourteen classes for the most part. However, they tried their best to impart whatever knowledge they had to us.

The teaching style at my school was quite outdated. There was a blackboard on the front wall, on which the teachers would write with chalk. They would fill the board and ask us to copy from there. Sometimes, they explained something on the board and made illustrations or gave examples. During the math class, the teacher would solve problems on the board and gave some as the homework.

A lot of them would ask us to read from the textbook; hence, there were regular reading drills. Passing from the corridor, anybody could hear us reading some lines in a singsong manner. Sometimes, the teacher would pick one student to read aloud, and the others would follow with their eyes on the book. After some time, he would take the seat, and somebody would continue from where he stopped. Reading was more like a ritual to us.

Out of all the subjects we had, mathematics was my favourite. I looked forward to Math class. It was thrilling to solve mathematical questions. Perhaps I had a thing for numbers or calculations because I enjoyed doing math and would never get bored with it. It was my math notebook that received the most commendable remarks from the teachers. Interestingly, math is also my daughters' favourite subject. All three of them like math the most.

My school only had junior level education available at it. In order to get higher education, I had to move a bit far from my home to live in a hostel. High school was the beginning of a new chapter in my life. Whereas I rejoiced the prospect of acquiring higher education, little did I know that life had more challenges in store for me.

I had to live in a hostel to attend senior school. The daily commute to and from school did not change much in this new phase of life. Since the school was much far from the hostel, I had to walk a couple of miles on foot to reach the school and do the same back to the hostel.

My hostel was a small building with bare minimum facilities. Living in such as place meant increased responsibility. We shared rooms with each other and did our chores ourselves. I would attend school during the day and come back to the hostel to pick the piles of errands I needed to get done. I would wash my clothes all by myself and do the dishes as well. It was tough to manage work and studies together. I would barely get any time for homework. When done with all the chores, I'd pick up my books and study.

My parents were extremely fond of getting their children educated. It was their biggest dream to see us all qualified and settled in our lives. They believed education was the key to success and prosperity. They had seen the hard life of a farmer, and they knew how difficult it was to survive despite working all through the day. They eagerly wanted their children to pursue a respectable career with higher earning prospects.

My brother Bhikhu was already working toward achieving that dream. He would work tremendously hard at his studies. He had adopted my parents' dream of becoming an educated man and inspired me to do the same. Unfortunately, fate had it otherwise, and I could not pursue higher studies. I completed grade 12, after which I started trying my hands with business because I had to earn money.

My reasons for quitting my studies were simple. I did not know the English language and had to start way behind others. In that way, I would have to spend many years before being able to read and write properly. I did not have that much time. I needed to start making money. Hence, I made the tough decision of putting a stop to my studies and started working.

I am a huge proponent of education. I stand for the rights of everybody to acquire quality education. Educated minds are enlightened minds. Therefore, I wanted my daughters to graduate from a university and make a career for themselves. I got my daughters admitted to a school, supported their education, and made sure they get to the university, which they did. The time when they were studying at school was tight for our family in terms of finances. We, nonetheless, kept pushing them for education because we had our priorities clear.

Looking back, I realise that neither the education I got nor the experiences I had at the school could not equip me with the skillset or expertise required to earn a respectable livelihood. Hence, I had to struggle a lot to make something out of myself. At the same time, I feel perhaps life had other ways of rewarding me as it offered me multiple opportunities for a better future. I feel contented that I eventually managed to grab the opportunities life threw at me and provide everything I didn't have to my daughters, including quality education.

Let's close this chapter with the pictures of my school.

Chapter 6: Farewell

One of the best things parents can do for their children is to provide them with a role model. The best-case scenario would be to become that role model themselves. Call it me lucky if you like that I had a mentor in my father. He was the prime example of the kind of man I wanted to become. My father did not leave any property or precious possessions behind, but he gave us his exemplar qualities, which helped me rise like a phoenix after severe setbacks later in life.

My father was a man of principles. He was an honest and upright individual. He would never bow before any material power at the expense of giving up on what was right and truthful. He would take the side of the rightful in any given situation. One of his overarching personality traits was that he was also a lionhearted man. He would not deter from calling a spade a spade. He spoke the truth without fearing the consequences.

He had been the chief of our village. In villages, there is a distinct legal system called *panchayat*. A *panchayat* is a group of highly respected and upright men who are the judicio-legal authority within the village. The head of the *panchayat* was called a *sarpanch* or *mukhiya*. These people were appointed with the consent of the villagers, and their decisions are binding on all and sundry.

The job of the council of elders was to decide cases among people. The villagers would bring all kinds of cases or disputes to the council. These could range from land disputes to personal disagreements between two parties. The panchayat would hear testimonies of both sides and make decisions based on rationality and experience.

My father was the mukhiya of the house for good five years. During this time, he heard multiple cases and resolved a number of interparty disputes. That position earned my father immense respect. He was known for making the right decisions in the face of opposition. Nobody could flatter him or pressurise him into making a decision in their way. He was known for never taking favours from anyone. What he wanted was justice, and nobody could make him from taking a just decision.

His determination was incorrigible. Ill doers were afraid of him because they knew my father wouldn't spare them. He exuded an aura of authority and uprightness. Wherever he went, people would accompany him for a discussion on business and other affairs. The villagers would gravitate toward him as metal gets attracted to the magnet. Such was the degree of charm in his personality.

My father was highly knowledgeable. He was an authority in farming and irrigation practices. People often came to him for suggestions, and he would not think twice before offering help in any way he could. Whenever he came to know of someone's suffering, he would approach them and offer his support. When asked for guidance in any matter, my father wouldn't refuse. He was like a father figure to not just his children but also to many other people who looked up to him.

My father spoke with authority, weighing his words before speaking. When he talked, everybody else listened. He exercised absolute command over speech. He was eloquent and self-assured. When he explained something, he would do that by giving examples and illustrations and made his point effectively. He never talked idly; his arguments were always backed by evidence.

My father had an influential personality in every sense of the word. He was known by everybody in the village as a rightful man. Even today, when I meet the people of Kaliari, they have only praises and respect for my father. What is more surprising is that the children of the village tell me the feats of my father which they have heard from their parents or grandparents. My father might be no more in this world, but he has left a legacy in the village.

As a farmer, my father was very hardworking. He would never shirk work. He started his day at five in the morning and worked till the evening. He would spend all his day and the farm looking after the crops. If anything was off, he would go the extra mile to fix it. While dealing with a challenging task, he would never take no for an answer. It was as if he knew he would accomplish the task; only he had to find how. He would try one method, then another, and finally, achieve what he wanted to.

While dealing with people, he would negotiate with them so effectively that they couldn't help agree to his demands. He had a robust and convincing tone. Since he was always on the side of truthfulness and honesty, he wouldn't give up his position in the face of setbacks. He had taught us all to fight for our rights and achieve what we want with belief in ourselves and never to give up our position no matter what.

I was fortunate to have spent a lot of time with my father. My daily routine involved visiting the farm and supplying things my father asked me for. Some of the days, I would get him lunch and spend the rest of the day with him. I would observe him keenly. Thanks to spending quality time with my ideal, my father, I learned plenty of skills. I wished his outstanding qualities would rub off on me, and I became his clone in terms of the skills and traits he possessed.

Today, if I am good at dealing with people, negotiating with them, convincing the other party to cut a deal, it is all because of my father. Not just that, I am also an upright and honest individual because my father brought me up to be one. I have the habit of working hard at the goal I have set my eyes to, and that is one of the most pricy habits I have acquired from my father.

One summery day, I was coming back from school after taking the exam. It was the summer season, during which came our midterm exams. After that, we would go on long vacations. Like the other kids, I was looking forward to the holidays and was carving different plans in anticipation thereof. It was a typical day. We woke up at five. I quickly completed my chores for the day and glanced through the books and notebooks to revise the contents before the exam.

During exam days, our school would close earlier. I got free around 10:30 and walked my way home. I knew my father would be waiting for me to come. I hurried on my way to reach home early, thinking my father would be waiting for me to lunch together. Around 11 o clock, I arrived home, and as soon as I entered the front door, I heard a loud noise followed by a thud upstairs. My breath stopped for a moment, and I rushed upstairs to check on my father.

Upon reaching there, I found him lying with his back on the floor. His eyes were closed, and he looked motionless. My heart was pumping ten times faster than normal at that moment. A 12 years old lad had little idea what to do when they found somebody lying static on the floor. I rushed to him and gently put his head on my lap. I was shouting at the top of my lungs, calling for help, calling the names of our neighbours, hoping somebody would come and see what's wrong with my father.

The old wooden house perhaps blocked my voice. Hence, I put my father's head back and came running down the stairs and outside the house. I would shout, "somebody, please come. Help my father. He's god unconscious. Take him to the hospital. Call a doctor." Those were all the words I could muster to speak. My yelling was heard by many people who entered the house and rushed towards the room where my father was.

In the next few minutes, a chorus had surrounded my father's body. They began examining him in their own ways. Somebody took his hand and checked his pulse. Somebody put brought their hands to his nose and see if he was breathing. Somebody else would touch his feet to check the level of warmth in them. My mother had gone to see a relative in the hospital. Somebody asked to bring her back hurriedly.

The villagers had called a doctor. From what I remember, the doctor checked my father and went outside. In those days, it was a tradition not to talk about the patient's situation or death in front of the kids. Hence, the doctor and some elderly villagers were talking silently in the corner, and I could not make anything out of their conversation. I was told that my father was sleeping and that he would wake up any minute.

The 12-year-old me was under the impression that my father had gone unconscious. I thought somebody would call a doctor, and he would check my father. My head was weaving thoughts of a couple of days ahead. I imagined my father waking up from deep slumber. I was planning to give him complete rest. I would not let him work extra hard at the cost of his health. I'd take him for regular check-ups, and in a few days, he would be back to normal. I did not know neither my father nor my life was going to be normal from now on.

When all of that was going on, people started talking silently with one another in an aggrieved manner gesturing at my father. I was too naïve to take the signal. But it was not long before I realised what had happened. After some time, my mother came into the house and began crying in anguish, looking at my father's body. Her body could not bear the burden of this painful sight, and she fell down by my father, crying her eyes out.

It was at that moment that the truth dawned upon me. I realised, "My father is no more in this world". My life had come to a standstill. I could not bear the burden of losing my father. It was almost as if the sky had fallen upon us. Our lives turned upside down from that day on. Nothing was going to be the same. My father, the head of our family and a paragon for us had bid adieu to this world. I was an orphan now at the young age of 12 with the responsibility of looking after my mother.

I was in a state of shock upon learning about my father's demise. You could slap me, hit me in the gut, push me on the floor or drag me in the streets; I wouldn't feel anything. The person I had loved and admired the most had gone. My world had fallen apart. I couldn't explain how I felt on that day and in the days to come. I did not want to accept the fact that my father had passed away.

On the night before his funeral, we sat around his body, taking some final glances at him. It was our last night together. That was perhaps the first time in my life when I hadn't eaten in 24 hours, and I did not feel hungry. My body had stopped perceiving any sensations. I was so desolate that I could not comprehend what was happening around me. All I could see was my father's corpse lying before us, lifeless.

63

My father's death was a huge shock for us, partly because he was not old and partly because he had no history of diseases. He was not under any sort of medication. He looked absolutely okay and performed all the functions perfectly well. By appearance, he was perfect. He was lean, did not have excess fat on his body, and never complained of any illness. We could not think in the wildest of our imagination that my father would depart from the world this soon. But it was true, and we had little choice than to accept it.

Soon after, the preparations for my father's funeral began. They clad my father in a white shirt and pair of white pyjamas after bathing him one last time. His nostrils were stuffed with cotton, and his feet tied together with a piece of white cloth. They put his body in the middle of the floor, surrounded by people from the village, our relatives, my brothers, and my mother.

One by one, people would come and mourn for my father's death. They would make my mother wail over and over again by reminding her of the loss. My father's picture was taken off the wall to put a garland around it. Wreaths were put around the pictures of the deceased. That reminded us that he was no more in this world.

There was a *pandit*, spiritual leader, at our home to assist us in performing the last rites of my father. He guided us to carry out the tasks one by one, and we followed. After the ceremonies finished, we lifted him up and carried his body to the crematory ground, *shamshan ghath*, with other relatives and villagers following the procession. Only the male members were allowed to go to the crematory ground. My mother stood back, wailing on the front door as we departed with the body.

In the shamshan ghath, there were wooden logs ready to accommodate his body. We put him on them and performed some last prayers. That was the last time ever that we got to see my father's face. After that, his face was covered with a white sheet, and his body was put on fire. The most beloved person in my life was burning to ashes before my eyes, and I could only stand there and witness the last signs of him disseminating into the air.

As part of the ritual, my mother had to wear a white sari now that she was a widow. She was not allowed to don any embellishments or wear colourful clothes from now on. If she did, it meant a breach of sacred laws. The belief in our culture was that a widow had no right to look appealing or enjoy herself because all her happiness was attached to her spouse. When he had died, there was no point in her grooming herself. She was supposed to look like a bereaving widow all the time and mourn for the loss of her husband till her last breath.

My father's death was the beginning of a tragic period in our life. When the head of the family was no more with us, society attacked us brutally, throwing its outdated conditions and exposing their ugly faces to us. Life was normal for very few days after my father's departure. We did not expect things would take a turn for the worst this quickly, but such is life.

Chapter 7: The Next Five Years

If I was asked to name the worst time of my life, I would, without a single thought, mention the time when my father died. The year 1975 was a turning point in my life. It was the terrible year that took my father away from us. The time surrounding his death passed without us realising what was happening around us for a couple of days. My father's funeral ended, people came and condoned his death, and that's all.

People went on with their affairs, and in a matter of days, we were left to ourselves. The next five years were a real struggle. Perhaps struggle is a mild word to describe our experiences. The distress and the challenges we faced in order to put food on the plate were agonising to extreme degrees.

My father was like the roof to us; he'd protect us from harsh weather and cruelties of the world outside. Now that he was no more, we had lost the roof, with no finances to meet our expenses. It took us about six months to get our thoughts together and accept that our father wasn't there anymore. Perhaps we would never admit that reality if it weren't for a plethora of financial challenges staring us in the eyes. The reality almost jolted us out of our denial and shook us to the very core. By that time, my two brothers had returned to my uncles' villages and my mother and I were left in the conundrum.

After my father's funeral, a man from the neighbourhood came to our home. *"Your father took some money from me before he passed away. I want my money back."* My mother and I were taken aback at the revelation. We did not know if my father had borrowed any money from this man. He never shared anything with us. So, we strode to where he kept his books and searched them for any mention of a loan involving this man.

We did not find any. Only God knows if that man was speaking the truth. However, we could not refuse somebody standing at our door demanding his money back, partly because we did not know the whole truth and partly because we were just not in a position to refuse a man who was ten times more respectable than a widow. I was a boy, and my mother was now a widow. We had no value in the sight of the villagers. So, we somehow arranged the amount and got it off our chest.

If that was not enough, some other people came to our house. Then there were more asking for money they lent for my father's funeral. When it happened, we were not in our senses. We did not know how much amount was paid by whom. Now that they were demanding their money back, we found ourselves in a quicksand. Every day, new faces appeared at our door, wanting their money returned at the earliest.

Arranging money for the lenders was the biggest of the many challenges we faced. We had no clue what we were going to do next. Hence, we thought it better to sell some of our animals and some household materials to get some money quickly and pay off the debt. We had only one source of income, and that was our farm. Whatever money came from there was stretched to last the entire time before the next produce. Now that my father was not there, we had to focus our attention on our only source of income.

Even though my father had a farm, but nobody amongst us knew the ins and outs of farming. *"How were we going to survive?" "Where is the next meal going to come from?"* became nagging concerns. On top of that, we weren't grown up, experienced farmers; we were only three juveniles, two of which lived far from the hometown. I was the only natural choice when it came to running the house.

As for my mother, she had remained a housewife all her life. She had no idea as to how the farm functioned or how crops were grown. My mother would hardly ever step outside of the four walls of our house, as per the customs of Indian village society. At most, she would go to our relatives or a handful of neighbours. She had visited the farm but never worked there. Our society would not allow women to work alongside men; neither did I want my mother to go through that struggle at the age that she was in.

With no other option, I rolled up my sleeves and got my feet wet with farming. In the initial period, we faced so many difficulties on the farm regarding minor tasks. Every time I started doing it, one problem or the other popped up before my eyes. Sometimes, I did not know which fertilisers to use. Other times, I wasn't sure if I was doing crop rotation the right way.

Many a time, I found myself going up to people to seek help. However, people didn't always advise me properly. In fact, some deliberately gave the wrong advice to cause us damage. During those trying times, three great men came to the rescue. Since they didn't know anything apart from farming, they offered a pair of hands. They had previously been doing farming with my father for a long time then. They helped us with fertilisers, crops, timing, and methodologies. To this day, I'm extremely grateful for their sincerity and dedication.

These humble men were a prime example of what it meant to be loyal. As they say, good deeds last long. My father had gone from the world, but his deeds stayed around.

He had helped these men some time back, and that translated into us getting assistance from them when we needed it the most. I would always be indebted to them for their assistance during the most gruelling times of our lives.

Doing farming all by ourselves was very difficult. We could barely have enough to arrange for the basic meals through farming. As soon as the produce matured, I'd rush to sell it so that I could put some money on my mother's hands. A couple of months would pass by, and we would run out of money. We had two options then. The first was to wait for the next crop money, but we needed something to live on till the next harvest. The other option was to go and knock on people's door for a loan. We had to go with this one.

Farming was not a promising source of income. We'd sow two crops on our farm, rice in monsoon and mango trees in the summer. When rice yield was good, mango would give a poor harvest, and if mangoes were abundant, rice production would be lower. That is how it went on for the most part. There were very few times when we got good harvests for both. In those times, we could fill our baskets with food for the whole year. Unfortunately, that was a rare case.

My mother one day emptied the grocery boxes to collect the last bit of grains left. In dismay, she said, *"Shashi, we* have no money left to buy more food. *This much here won't last very long"*. A young boy of twelve years old had never experienced a predicament worse than that. I'd ask my mother, *"What do we do now?"*. She would respond with a heavy heart, *"We'd have to ask someone for money until the next produce"*. *"But who do we go to?"* I had no idea.

My mother sent me to a couple of relatives. I would go to their homes, knock on the door, in the meanwhile, summon enough courage to ask for money. I spoke to them politely, expecting help from their end. The response from some people shocked me, *"When will you return it?"* I would often find myself struggling for words in such situations before stammering a response, *"We'll return it as soon as we get the money from our next harvest"*.

Not all the people I went for help acted in the same manner. A couple of relatives were really kind to us. In fact, they would help us on a regular basis. They never raised the questions as to when and how we were going to return the money. They knew my father and enjoyed cordial relations with him. They had a firm belief in our values and possessed a kind heart. I'd thank them they generously said, *"It's fine. If you need more, you can come back to us"*.

There were some other people who slammed the door in my face. Our asking money would bother them. These were the people whose attitude was all soft and nice when my father was alive. Now, they would act as if we didn't exist.

Asking for money was not a one-time thing. Nobody, no matter how generous, could give us enough money to last long. Therefore, we had to think of other people we could go up to. It was humiliating, to say the least. The more I asked for money, the more I felt the burning desire to stand on my own two feet.

Now I knew how difficult a task dealing with finances was. It became all the more difficult when the finances were depleting, and there was no other stream of income in sight. Things became bleaker because the finance manager was a twelve years old child with no prior experience handling loans. Every interaction was marked by an underlying fear, *"what if they didn't lend you money?"*. Some people, out of fear of losing money, began avoiding us in the first place.

One of the most painful sights in this world is that of a mother weeping in front of her child. I had seen that quite frequently. My mother would often cry at night, worrying where the next meal would come from. It tore me into a million pieces. I loved her dearly, but all I could say was, "Don't worry mum. Everything will be alright". Often times, we had conversations about money before going to bed. Our heads were occupied with only one thing – money.

My relation with those my age changed after my father passed away. I wouldn't play with them anymore. I couldn't have fun; I couldn't laugh when my mother was shedding tears. I was always occupied with thoughts of relieving her. My childhood had ceased there and then. What else could I do was the question I asked myself. I couldn't open my heart to anybody, and I couldn't enjoy anything because I wasn't sure if we would have the next meal.

At twelve years old, when a normal boy of my age would be busy focusing on his education, I was stressing out over farm-related tasks correctly, arranging for the bread and butter of my family, and covering the debts. All the time in school, I would be thinking about managing the finances. Education was not a panacea to my problems. I needed money. That too, instantly. I could not wait to get a degree in some ten years time and began earning.

Getting education was definitely not the way out for me. It would take me too long to get money into the house. And time was the problem. I was running out of time to help my family financially. However, there was no solution in sight. I couldn't think of getting to a place where I could make ample money since I did not know any valuable skill at that time.

One day I sat with my mother and shared the details regarding all the loans we had to pay off. I asked her, *"should we contact my brothers?"*. She immediately responded, *"No, they're studying. Let them focus on their education. I don't want to disturb them"*. My mother could never think of informing my brothers of our plight, no matter how worse it got. She wanted them to get an education and build a career out of it.

Whenever any of my brothers called, they would ask how things were going at our end. My mother's words rang in my ears, and I'd assure them, *"Everything is okay, here. We're good"*. We never revealed the actual picture to them. It was pleasing to see them getting ahead in their lives, even if it meant more responsibility on my shoulders.

The feeling of not being able to help my family get out of this problematic and mortifying situation made me feel so small. I was like a stone lying on the road, valueless. Anybody could come and tread over us. We had absolutely no value in the eyes of people. It was natural. Nothing in this world comes for free. When you ask favours, you are losing your esteem, your importance, and your say in all matters. You become no more than an object for people.

Being poor and without a father meant you had to take all the blame for anything wrong that happened in your vicinity. In my village, for example, the *sarpanch* would hold me accountable for things I never did. One time, somebody accused me of theft, and the case was taken to the *sarpanch*. The head of the council ruled the decision against me. They knew I had nobody to protect me and that they could use me as a scapegoat for ill doings of other people.

When my mother got to know about it, she was grossly upset. She began beating me in a state of anger, disappointment, and fear. She was afraid that could bring a bad name to the family. Knowing that my father was not there to support us, she had a hard time dealing with such situations. The only thing she had in her hands was fixing my behaviour. That she did in her own way, whereas I kept pleading for innocence.

If we weren't poor, we wouldn't have faced such a shameful time at the hands of society. We stayed in this vicious cycle of poverty for about five years and kept receiving humiliation day in and day out. Poverty is a menace. Debt is a bigger menace. Once you take it, you will have to count on it over and over again.

It was absolutely harrowing to beg for money time and again. The money we got would be used by the time the next produce came out. The money we got from this one would be budgeted into multiple small portions, such as payoffs, ration budget, school fee, etc. We would be keeping a huge chunk aside for paying back loans. After this chunk was eliminated from the gross pool, we were again left with insufficient money to survive. The only result was to borrow more money.

My father never prepared me for financial work. It was when he was no more in this world that we realised how difficult it was to make both ends meet. It required so much courage, so much drudgery to manage the finances. This massive responsibility that fate had put on my shoulders made me grow faster than other kids of my age.

I was at least ten years ahead of my age, judging by a measure of duties I'd perform. My circumstances made me a responsible adult. The lessons I learned during those five years remained with me for a lifetime and the dreadful memories I made in that time kept haunting me for years.

Chapter 8: New Beginnings

The time from the age of twelve to seventeen was taxing, to say the least. I faced unlimited issues, discrimination, and prejudice in my village. No single day would pass without us worrying about making both ends meet. Life became so uncertain that, at times, we did not know where our next meal would come from. My mother and I would share our grief and cry ourselves to sleep some nights.

Things were pretty much the same until there came a time when my brother was getting married. By this time, he was an educated man with the certification of chartered accountancy under his belt. He got a good marriage prospect. My sister in law was born in India and raised in the UK. She was very educated herself and was a kind and humble soul. I was super happy to see my brother getting married to such a wonderful woman.

Generally, the wedding was a grand function for the people. It was supposed to be celebrated with all the zeal and zest. There would be lots of people thronging to wedding halls or tents. Those were decorated with lights, flowers, and colourful curtains. Some people would call artists to beat drums and blow the trumpet. Young boys and girls would dance to Bollywood songs. There would be special arrangements for the bride and groom, who were expected to do a number of rituals with all cheers and laughter.

It was special fun for the bride and groom's family and friends. There would be a competition between the two while performing the rituals, with each surrounded by their supporters. However, we did not have the resources for a grand wedding. Therefore, we could not make opulent arrangements. Just a few people attended the wedding, and that was all.

My sister in law's family came to India for the wedding ceremony. There were 20 people on each side. It was a simple function, involving the bride and groom flinging garlands around each other's necks and taking the *pheray*, seven rounds around the fire, with the *pundit* saying the prayers. My brother applied *sindoor* along the parting line of his wife's hair and tied the *mangalsutra* around her neck. Together, these are the signs of a married woman, *suhagan*.

Soon after the wedding, my brother left for the UK along with his wife. Upon reaching England, he busied himself in the process of sponsoring my mother and me to the UK as well.

"*How are you doing?*" he asked on the call.

"We are good."

"Good to know that. Here's good news for you. I have applied for your immigration. I want you and mother to come here and live with us."

I was optimistic about the prospects of living in the UK since I had heard a lot of majestic things about it. Most of all, I wanted to leave Kaliari. There was no future for us in there. We could not improve our circumstances; we were going with the flow of life, and there was no way we could escape the cycle.

We needed to get a lot of paperwork to be done for immigration. Hence, I arranged for a bus ticket and started off for Mumbai along with my mother. Mumbai is the biggest city in India. It is also the place where all the important buildings and offices are. We went to the office of the High Commissioner to proceed with official work.

It took some time for the clearance. We received our passports from the office. Now, we were ready to go to the UK. My mother and I started packing with excitement. We put our little belongings into the bag with the pictures of my father and left for the airport.

Call it a coincidence if you like; our departure was on 15th August 1980. It the same day when India got independence. Every year, millions of Indians celebrate this day with lots of fervour. They raise Indian flags, paint their faces the colour of the flag, and dance to the tune of national songs to commemorate the day. From that year on, this was going to be my independence day too. I was going to be released from the clutches of my inherently bad circumstances. My fate was going to change.

Just before leaving, I met a couple of close friends and got my mother to meet a few of hers. We did not see many people, as most were not on good terms with us. When the plane took off, I felt a weighty object easing off my chest. I had not had this feeling in a long time. We were going to get rid of poverty, humiliation, and debtors, who'd leave no stone unturned to insult us. We were going to be free at last.

As exciting as it was, travelling to the UK was no less challenging. The challenge laid in going through the entire process, from getting the documents for immigration made to boarding the plane and landing safely at the UK airport. These menial tasks seemed difficult because I could not speak English. Hence, I took the help of a family friend to guide me beforehand. He taught me a couple of phrases I could use if nothing else worked.

On landing at the UK airport, I was relieved in the true sense of the word. The UK presented a picture totally opposite to my homeland. This country looked clean. There was no garbage on the streets, unlike in India. On my way to my brother's home, I kept glancing at the tidy houses and immaculate gardens with amazement. The stores were organised, with special attention given to packaging and cleanliness. In India, we had shops with unkempt shopkeepers selling different items. Many a time, they would have eatables exposed to the air, attracting flies and others insects.

The people in this part of the world were more educated, cultured and civilised. They would abide by the rules, and most of them would know the rules, to my surprise. Back in India, you could not expect people to know what was right or wrong. Most of them would just consider themselves right in the event of a conflict.

Here, everything was so systematic. It was almost as if I had entered a new world. One of the first things that impressed me in the UK was the road sense people displayed. People would drive in a disciplined manner with hardly any horns to be heard while you're on the road. In India, on the other hand, everybody would peep the horns every 30 seconds or so. You could not possibly travel without your ears getting numb by all the noise.

I lived for a couple of days with my brother, and the realisation dawned upon me, *"This world is full of opportunities. There is no established system, like in Kaliari. Here, you could rise above the ladder if you make sufficient attempts. It boils down to how hungry you are to avail the opportunities."* I saw people doing manual work and making a good deal of money. I came across shopkeepers earning huge numbers in pounds. I even bumped into people who weren't very educated, but they were making good money and even sending some to their relatives living in India.

This place had a lot in store for people like me. I just needed to figure out where to put my energy and work hard. Money would automatically follow. My destiny was in my hand because I was in a place where hard work would not go in vain. The more efforts I put into work, the more rewards I would get.

I had two options for me, stay here and make a fortune, or go back to India and continue living the life I was living. The harsh memories of me tiring myself to work and begging for loans in front of people came back rushing across my mental slate. I would not wish that life upon anybody. The memories were bitterly painful, and there was no question of going back to India.

My brother was concerned about my future. He had a thoughtful conversation with me. *"Shashi, what do you want to do now?"* he would ask me.

I responded without thinking for the second time, *"Business"*.

"You don't want to complete your education first?"

"No. I have gotten enough degrees from my previous school. Now what I need the most is money. I cannot spend more time getting an education when I could use the same for earning money".

"Okay, if that is your decision, I respect it. But to do anything, you'll have to learn English first."

"Yes! That's probably where I should start from."

Till this time, I could not understand a single word of English. In order to do anything in this land, I needed to learn their language first. As for education, I was in no way against it. I did not pursue it for a reason. My chances of acing at college were abysmally low since I was not starting from where everybody else started. I was way behind them.

Covering that distance would take me years. Why should I put extra time into acquiring education when I could utilise the same to earn money?

I took admission in an English language course offered by a lady free of cost. It did help me in getting the hang of the basics. The lady was teaching in a traditional way. Some of the lessons helped, some did not. In about six months time, I left and geared up for work, knowing that the rest I would learn on the job. Languages could not be learnt without practice.

Thanks to my natural predisposition to absorbing knowledge from my environment, I was able to learn how things worked in the UK pretty fast. I had an innate learning attitude towards everything in life. Even if I was walking by the street, I would notice the ways people greeted one another. When I visited a shop, I would see how the business worked and how they dealt with the clients. When I passed by the bus stop, I would observe the ways people boarded onto it.

I would grasp knowledge from my surroundings. There was nothing of value that happened around me without me taking note of it and deriving lessons from it. By and by, I learned the ways people here communicated with one another. I noted how business affairs were managed here. The retail industry specifically attracted my attention.

In contrast to farming, business in the UK was a much better option. Farming was a long term investment. It would take as many as six months to get the crop. Business, on the other hand, would reap the profits much earlier. The profit and loss in farming depended on many natural factors, such as weather, diseases, pest attacks. In business, however, the natural conditions had a smaller role, and one's individual efforts played a much more significant part.

Similarly, I could earn more if I worked harder in business, whereas in farming, I had to work super hard, and the results would not go beyond a certain mark because the profit margin was more or less fixed. We would sell the crop for a fixed price, with little differences, and the rest was the job of the middlemen who would make a lot more money supplying the produce to the market.

The rules of business in a country as developed as the UK were based on justice and equality of opportunity. Back in India, farming was an uneven ground. The rules of it allowed little room for impoverished farmers to make good profits due to government regulations and the structure of the system, whereby they lacked the opportunity to go one step ahead on the ladder. There was no ladder. You were like a piece in the puzzle, small and replaceable, with no space for vertical movement.

I heard people around me wanting to go back to India and wondered why. As for myself, I never wanted to go back. Not even once did it occur to me that I should return to my homeland. I knew life was going to be super hard in the UK. There would be nights when I'd have to sleep on an empty stomach, but I knew for sure that no matter what, the coming days would bring prosperity. There were opportunities that remained inaccessible in India, and I would try them with all the energy I had. Yes, there would be a lot of struggle, but did I not struggle as a farmer? Business wouldn't be easy, but was farming easy? It would be time taking, but then farming is a lot more strenuous and time-consuming. I had nothing to lose here.

I was laser-focused on making money. I had seen what poverty could do to you. I had experienced humiliation, distress, hunger, and whatnot at the hands of society due to poverty. That is why I was dead fixed on making money. The only immediate goal in my sight was to earn money, lots of it.

As for missing India, there was nothing I could possibly miss. My entire world comprised my family, my mother and my brothers. And they were there with me in the UK. There was nothing in my hometown that I could miss. I had the warmth of my mother's lap on which I could put my head when tired. I had the supporting arm of my brother that I could hold when life got uncertain. I had a congenial home environment in which we could celebrate our small achievements in our own way. My life was complete; I did not miss anybody.

My mother was delighted at the prospects of living in the UK. She did not have the burden of running the house or paying debts on her shoulders anymore. We, brothers, took it upon ourselves to arrange the finances. We made her retire right after landing in the UK. Even though I encountered many difficulties in increasing my income, I was not poor anymore. I would bring some money home and whatever I earned went to my mother because she had strived hard to raise us.

My mother lived in the UK for about 20 years before her demise. Those 20 years were carefree and jubilant days for her. We often took her out because she had hardly experienced any sort of amusement in her life. I even took her to movies. I could do anything to put a smile on her face. She got to spend a lot of time with my family and that of my brother. We were lucky to have our kids raised under her prestigious guidance.

Looking back, I realise life has its own way of rewarding us. We, on our part, need to be vigilant of opportunities. Once we come across one, there is no reason why we should not grab it. Perhaps your circumstances may not be in your favour, but you need to have the ability to put in all adequate hard work and keep going until you have achieved what you aimed for.

Chapter 9: Love

Love has different definitions for different people. For me, it meant living together and treading on the paths life opened up for you together. I did not get a chance to fall in love with anybody in my life back in India or even in the United Kingdom. Life kept me so busy that love barely crossed my mind. Perhaps a better way to put it would be, 'fancy notion of love never came into my mind'. I was too bent on making both ends meet and establishing a solid financial base that I did not think about anything else boys of my age fantasised.

Back at the store, I would be working day in and out. I often sat down for a few minutes, and in my reverie, I would imagine a girl helping me doing the work at the store. I thought to myself, "How nice it would be to have my life partner working side by side with me". I was quite sure that I wanted to get married, not for romantic reasons, but because I needed an extra pair of hands at work. What better way there was than to get married? And get married to somebody who would stand by me through thick and thin and who would also share my vision for life.

I was 19 when I decided to get married. It was a pretty young age for marriage in those days too. People poured in all kinds of comments and suggestions, starting from *"This was too much of responsibility"* to *"Marriage was not a joke"* and *"I should get stable enough before bringing another mouth to feed into the family"*. But I knew I needed a partner and that we would construct our world together.

Even though I was young, I was already responsible enough to take up a wife and look after her. And together, we would establish our business and at some point later start a family too. I discussed the idea with my mother and my brother, and they had no problems with me getting married. My mother expressed her opinion in the most comforting manner, *"It's your life, Shashi. If you want to get married, I have no issues with that."*

I never found myself a girl in the UK. One reason was that it never came into my mind that I should. Another was that I didn't have sufficient money to spend on girls. Yet another reason was that somebody outside of my culture, with a different background, would probably never understand my situation and perhaps never share my ambitions. For me, however, business and career were the main things.

I passed on the word to a couple of relatives about marriage. One of my cousins conveyed he knew a girl close to my age and from the same background as me. He suggested I asked for her hand in marriage. He showed me her photo and asked me for a picture of mine to be sent to her. Today, girls and boys meet one another in a fancy restaurant and choose their life partner after a lot of meetings, discussions, and deliberations. I chose my life partner in a very different manner.

My cousin showed me her photo. I saw a pretty girl, donning a plain *sari*, with a *bindi* on her forehead and a beautiful smile on her face. She looked wonderful. I was so happy to see this girl, and I couldn't stop wondering if she looked this beautiful in reality as well. My mother and brother saw the photo too. I desperately waited for my mother's response. She put her hand on my shoulder and said, *"I'm happy, Shashi if you are happy."* That nod was the approval I was looking forward to.

I did not inquire a lot about this girl because I was in such a hurry to get married. I sufficed with whatever information I got. I was told that she had three more siblings, and she was the oldest one. What mattered the most to me was that she was from India. She professed the same values as me. She practised the same culture and traditions as my family. It was also important for me that she was from a similar financial background as us.

Perhaps if I had married somebody from a wealthier background, she would never have understood my plight.

Also, that girl would want me to spend on her affluently, or maybe she had a different financial philosophy. She would perhaps not be interested much in saving money or making a career diligently. Those were the conflicts I wanted to avoid at all costs because I was hell bound on taking my business to new heights. So, I knew this girl was the ideal match for me.

We agreed to the marriage, and the word passed on to the girls family through my cousin. There was a small celebration in the family. I had chosen my life partner. Back in the days, there was no way we could communicate with one another. For one thing, it was not considered very nice. For another thing, we did not have those quick telecommunication mediums we have today. Having a conversation at that time would mean striding to the telephone booth, inserting a coin, and requesting to the receiver at the other end of the line to put up my fiancé on the line.

This was the time when telephones weren't available everywhere. Even if I arranged a phone, there was no point since my wife didn't have a telephone set back in India. Hence, I would either call a relative of hers who could call her to their place in turn. Alternatively, I could contact the nearest store in India that had the phone and request them to put up my fiancé on the line. How would I know my wife would be available when I called? One way was to set up a time beforehand and then make a call around that time. But to do that, there had to be some kind of a communication medium between us.

The easiest and simplest course of action was to avoid making any contact and meet her live. In the next six months, I sponsored her to come to the UK in the capacity of a fiancé. We also arranged some money to pay for her flight and other immigration expenses.

The day finally arrived when my fiancé was coming to the UK. I was going to see her for the first time at Heathrow airport. I remember a slim, pretty girl with black hair, a pointed nose, and a pair of big eyes from the picture. This same face I was looking for among a horde of passengers coming out. My eyes scanned the crowd until they rested upon this girl who looked a lot like my fiancé. There she was. Ten times more stunning than she looked in the photo. My lips spread in a big smile. At that moment, I had the first bit of romantic emotions rushing through my blood.

We greeted each other, and I noticed she had a beautiful voice too. She was a little shy and had bright eyes. She would talk softly, weighing her words before she spoke. I developed a deep liking for her, and even though we hadn't married yet, I started to think of her as my responsibility. I asked her how she was and if she had a good journey to the UK. She responded in affirmative quite shyly. That broke some ice between us, and we began talking.

I asked her, *"You'd be doing wedding preparations on your own?"*

"I'd do them with the help of my cousin."

"You must be needing some money for the wedding expenditure?"

She responded with, *"Oh! I'd borrow some from my relative for now."*

"No. You aren't taking any money from anyone. You are my responsibility now."

I immediately handed her some money I had saved from the store's earnings and told her to buy whatever things she needed for herself with it. Despite not being in a brilliant financial shape myself, I had already assumed her responsibility, for she was going to be my wife, my better half.

Just a few hours ago, I was riding the coach to my cousin's place, who was my wife's brother in law and then we went to the airport from there. Next, we took the bus back to our place. We couldn't afford to rent a car. Such was our financial condition. However, inside my heart, I was contented. I was overwhelmed with the reassurance that I had chosen the right life partner.

Within four weeks of her arrival in the UK, we got married. It was a very small function with 50 people from each side. Since this was in the UK, things were much more expensive than in India. So, we went for minimal food, a very basic celebration, and a handful of people as guests. That was all we could arrange the money for. But what mattered more was not how grand the celebration was but how two souls combined into one over a couple of magical vows.

Generally, couples plan for a honeymoon right after their marriage. They believe it is the ideal time to get to know each other and to create memories. I thought otherwise. I didn't feel the need for a honeymoon. My reasoning was we could utilise this time to make money and get rich. Once we had a lot in our accounts, we could go on as many honeymoons as we wished. In the line of that thought, I shunned the idea of a honeymoon, and my wife agreed with me.

The best thing about our marriage was that my wife shared my vision of life in almost every matter. I had plans to get this store running, after which I wanted to open more in other parts of the UK. I also wanted to invest in a business that I could take to the next level. All of that was not possible without a supporting spouse, and I was lucky to have that support system in the form of my wife. Both of us had experienced poverty quite closely, and that is why we were both inclined towards attaining financial independence first and foremost.

On the next day of our wedding, we both got up in the morning, had breakfast and went to the shop. It was our second day of marriage and first day at the store as Mr and Mrs Shashi. We were like two organs of the same body. We worked together, ate together, and in those moments of togetherness, we developed a deep fondness for each other. We were like a single entity. Soon enough, we became so dependent on each other that I could not imagine my life without her.

My wife couldn't speak or understand English. She belonged from a place in India where she didn't have good educational opportunities, and learning English was far from possible. So, naturally, I became her teacher. While dealing with customers, if she stuck somewhere, she'd consult me, and I'd explain it to her. She would ask me innocent questions like, *"What do we call this, Shashi?"*, *"Is this the vanilla flavour?"*, *"Where do I put this?"*. And I would be explaining to her, *"this is how you say this and that"*.

It was just after we had spent some time that I realised my wife had a big heart. She was not just a good wife, but a wonderful human being too. She treated my mother like her own. She would respect her, take her suggestions at home, ask for her blessings. She called her what I called her, *'Baa'*. I loved how the two most important women of my life bonded so well with each other. If somebody outside of our acquaintances had seen their bond, they would have thought of them more as mother and daughter than mother-in-law and daughter-in-law. That was how well they gelled in together, sharing their stories and interests like best friends.

Our family was small and we were closely knit together. We'd meet over lunch or dinner. Those were some merry moments we would have together. My wife got so well with my brother, my sister in law, and my mother that it felt as if she was made to be married into our family.

My wife was not just a good storekeeper; she was a super good cook too. She would watch my mother cooking and learn a number of recipes from her. This way, she got to know a lot of Indian dishes. She cooked food herself, did home chores, and made my home no less than heaven. She took so much interest in our business and home that every time I saw her, I felt so happy to have picked her up as my life partner.

Our bonding was perfect. We have a good understanding. At the age of 19, I was thinking like 35 years old. Often at night, we would sit together and make plans for the next fifteen years over a cup of tea. We would discuss the possible options before us. We'd make decisions together. It was our combined decision to save money for the future and spend less. We started every new chapter of our life after due discussions, and we never had difficulty reaching an agreement.

Much of the lessons for how to lead a successful married life were taken from my parents. I had always seen my parents having an excellent loving and caring relationship with each other. They would eat together, make decisions collectively, and support each other in all big and small matters. They loved and respected each other. I never remember my father raising his voice at my mother or my mother cursing my father or his family in a society where these things were not that much of a taboo. They made an ideal couple to me.

My wife and I were a lot like my parents. We would celebrate our festivals with full fervour. Money was not in abundant supply in the formative years of our marriage. However, we still made the best out of every moment in life. Some of our most struggling days seemed marvellous when we were together.

Typically, people meet their prospective life partners, spend time understanding them, fall in love with them and then get married. In our case, the sequence was a little different. We got married first, then spent time with each other, tried to understand each other, and then fall in love. Our love life was amazing. We enjoyed our lives together. Everything seemed beautiful with her by my side. To this day, we relish each other's company so much that we don't feel anything is missing from life when we are together.

Here are some pictures from our wedding day and early married life.

101

Chapter 10: Marriage

Lucky are those who have a lifestyle that affords them time to fall in love with someone. They enjoy going to movies with their romantic partners, go to parties, spend plenty of time together. Young boys and girls these days have it easy. Even if they don't experience courtships, they have the opportunity to have a couple of meet-ups with one another, with the help of which they get to know each other well.

In most of the weddings we attend these days, the couple is already familiar with each other. They already know so much about each other since they have had detailed conversations, thanks to social media. In our time, however, things were very different, and more so for us, considering our unique circumstances. I, for one, did not have the opportunity to have pre-marriage courtships, lunches, dinners or anything like that.

Our married life was very atypical. The start was very abrupt in terms of the ways our wedding was finalised and how our initial years went, but eventually, it turned supremely beautiful. Now when I look back at the past, I cannot help marvelling at how some things have an unusual start apparently, and they metamorphose to take a beautiful shape.

My marriage life was unique from the very start. Our engagement happened in a very novel manner than it takes place these days. There are huge parties, for example, guests are invented, expensive rings are exchanged, sumptuous dinner is arranged, and then there are photographs. People call professional photographers to capture those beautiful moments. In our case, we got engaged through photographs; that is, we just saw each other's photographs, and that was all about our engagement. No rings, no photoshoot, nothing of the sort took place.

Then came the time when our marriage was going to be finalised. Back in the days and in our culture, such things would take place in a very systematic, ritualistic manner. Where today, boys and girls meet each other, it was more of a family meet-up in our time. I remained in the UK, and my brothers and my mother went to Mina's, my wife's, uncle's place in Birmingham to fix the marriage and talk about the arrangements. They talked with my wife's family over the phone and set our wedding. They also discussed how the affairs would take place, such as how Mina would travel to the UK, where she would stay, how the marriage would take place, etc.

After Mina came to the UK, we were all set to be married in about two months time. In those two months, she lived at her uncle's house. Her parents could not come to the UK, so they just sent Mina there and were happy about the entire wedding. On our big day, we had only 25 guests from my side and about the same from hers. Interestingly, she had her uncle and cousins on her side only because her parents or siblings could not afford to travel to the UK.

Mina even did her wedding preparations with the help of her cousins and her uncle. The wedding preparations were not grand. She just bought a couple of dresses and accessories, and that was all. On our side, too, the arrangements were pretty simple. I just got myself a couple of nice clothes and some simple home accessories to get started with life as a married couple. We decorated our little home modestly with a few flowers to welcome the bride.

How things were happening at my wife's end deserves another explanation altogether. Since our proposal was recommended for marriage through a cousin, there was no question of doubting the other party. Trust was the most critical factor in relationships then. If somebody we were close with or somebody we trusted a lot vouched for an individual for marriage, we did not need to do any more verification. So, in our case, a very trusted cousin connected our families together, and that is how events leading to our marriage rolled on.

Mina, my wife, was only 18 years old at the time of our marriage. Just like me, she was extremely responsible for her age. Her responsibility had less to do with making both ends meet and more with keeping the family intact. She was a tremendously wise and responsible girl who was leaving her parents' house for a man she had only seen a photo of and who her parents had chosen as her life partner. Little did we know that she was going to make my world no less than heaven in the years to come.

Let me tell you how the talk of our marriage happened at her end. Back in the days, our culture did not offer a lot of room for women to have a say in their marriage. In villages particularly, families had a more conservative outlook of life. The elders would meet with the prospects and take the decision of marriage on their own. Boys did have some say, but girls hardly had any. In Mina's family, events progressed with the consent of the elders and when everything was finalised, Mina was informed about it.

She was told, *"Mina, we have fixed your wedding with Shashi."* However, since she had seen me in the picture and perhaps liked me too, she was satisfied with the decision. The only thing on her mind was how to make the marriage work because it was generally upon the girls to put their one hundred per cent into the marriage and make it a successful one. She was going to go abroad for the very first time to settle there. Mina was a little anxious, but she was confident in her own skin. She knew she would settle in the new lifestyle.

My mother in law briefed Mina on her upcoming life. She asked her to respect everyone in the family and outside, as Mina later told me. She asked her to take the responsibility of running the household and support my mother and me in everything we do, be it home chores or store work. Her words often rang in Mina's ears, *"Take my word upon it, Mina. You get what you give. If you want to get respect, you have to learn to give respect. If you want to get love, you have to offer it to your family first."* Those are the values she had sworn upon, and to this day, she observes them very closely.

Another important factor in our lives is destiny. We strongly believe whatever we get is written in our fate and that we have to put our fullest efforts into every relationship in life to make them more meaningful. That helped us get ready for whatever life had in store for us. With a firm belief in destiny, we took the leap of faith and got ready to embrace life with a complete stranger.

In our times, the joint family system was the best form of family structure. We could not imagine living separately in our village. There, people would not abandon their older parents or their siblings and lived comfortably together. Mina lived happily in the same system because she was pretty used to it. She had seen her parents living with their parents. Moreover, she was happy to have an elder in the family. She always thought a joint family worked better as you had more help from other people in the home. On that note, our values overlapped, and hence we never had any disagreements at any point later on.

That one element that made our marriage so successful was responsibility from the very beginning. It does the trick even when love is not the overriding factor in a relationship. That worked perfectly well in our case. On my side, I have already discussed in the previous chapters how much responsibility I had on my shoulders: the responsibility of being the breadwinner in the family, of looking after my mother's needs, of developing a stable financial base for the future, and of becoming independent so that we did not have to seek help from anybody ever.

It was not just me; Mina, too, had the responsibility of keeping the house intact and running. From a very young age, she was taught our core traditional values. She knew she did not have to let down anybody in the family. She would be there to look after everyone's needs. Being a woman and a wonderful human being, she understood the ups and downs my mother had experienced. Therefore, she made sure to give every comfort we could afford to my mother.

At the beginning of our married life, when money was not abundant, we made sure we get our mother to enjoy. We would go out with her, take her for meet-ups. My wife and my mother were always on the same page, so I did not have to choose between them. We decided our matters together as a family. Neither did my mother ever try to impose her will on our personal issues, nor did Mina ever challenged her in any way. They were always two happy women taking pride in their culture.

The spark of love the modern generation deems necessary today was not very much evident from the beginning in our relationship, where love grew with time. I did feel a rush of happy emotions upon seeing her at the Heathrow airport, but love in a true sense started quite late. I later got to know that she was delighted to see me too. She liked the way I looked, the way I behaved, and how I cared for her needs from the very start. Perhaps care and responsibility sow the seeds of love, and that love is eternal; it stays forever and keeps growing with every passing phase of life.

The time we got between her arrival in the UK and our wedding was the closest we came to dating. Our dates were not the ones where you would go out on dinners and have a loose talk. At most, we got to have a light chit chat on the phone. She had a phone set at her uncle's house. I would call her daily, and that got us to know each other better before formally starting the relationship. Most of our conversations revolved around routine matters, such as wedding preparations, family, work-life, etc.

People say friendship often forms the basis of love; chances of love to thrive are meagre when there is no friendship. That proved very authentic in our experience. Marriage bound us into a relationship of responsibility and care. Together, they engendered a never-ending friendship. In our new phase of life, we were experiencing the ups and downs together. I was teaching her English. I was growing as a person and was helping her to grow in her own capacity. We were exploring the world together. We were less like a married couple and more like friends. We would share our grief, crack jokes together, laugh our lungs out in each other's company, and experience life to the fullest.

When we experienced good times, we made sure to enjoy them together. When there were hard times, I would know for a fact that Mina was there for me, and she knew that I would never abandon her no matter what. In our culture, we have this ritual in weddings in which we get a knot tying us together while making the rounds, *phere*, around the fire. I feel that knot was so powerful; it tied us so close together that we cannot imagine our lives without each other today.

Today, you can lock us in a room and open us after hours, and we'd be happy. We enjoy each other's company so much that we don't need anybody else, just Mina and me. It is hard for others to believe that ours was an arranged marriage and that we did not know each other before. People have a hard time believing that love can exist between a retired couple. When they take my take on it, *"love has only ever grown between us with every passing day"*, they are usually taken aback. Such is the strength of our love and the nature of our relationship. I would definitely give a lot of credit to my better half for igniting such energy into our relationship and making it stronger than ever.

We have had our fair share of disagreements in life, but we never even once fought with each other. Not even once did we leave the other or stopped talking for days. We never broke the channels of communication between us. At most, we would disagree on minor issues and in the next twenty minutes, we would be seen talking to each other like nothing happened. Our children look up to us; we are their version of what an ideal couple looks like.

Oftentimes in life, you have to put others before you to make a relationship successful. That was my wife's and my mantra for life. We did groom ourselves and grew in our personal capacities with time, but we also never left the other members of the family alone. We put their needs first, and they reciprocated. The way to make your family life successful is to look after everybody so that they don't feel excluded. This is particularly true in a joint family.

As of writing this book, we have been happily married for 38 years. It makes me immensely proud to have a partner with whom I have the best level of understanding and who always stays by me at all times. As a married couple, we have seen extremely trying times in the form of financial difficulties and the death of my close ones, such as my mother and my middle brother. In those times, Mina was my constant support, and so was I for her.

On the other hand, we had experienced some of the most beautiful times, such as when my business took off, and we were financially strong. In those days, we made sure to stay together and enjoy our life in the best manner possible. It was also the time when I fulfilled the promises I made to her in the early days of our marriage. So, while I could not take her for a honeymoon right after marriage, we had many amazing vacations in the later years of our marriage.

Even today, Mina is my best friend, and I am hers. I now realise that the notion of love people often have in their minds can be misleading. True love involves care, responsibility, friendship, and understanding. Perhaps life cannot function in a normal way without these elements. When these are given, love comes about, as it did between us. That love, in my opinion, is everlasting; it only grows with time. A time comes when beauty fades, the energy goes down, but that love binds you together in an inseparable knot.

Chapter 11: Decisions, Decisions

Life is demanding. It does not offer you anything on a plate. Instead, it constantly puts you in situations where you will be forced to think, experiment, learn, unlearn, relearn, and go through a host of events to come to a decision. Big things in life require tough decisions to be made, and those decisions would not always be right; but you have to have faith and experiment. If you know in your heart that you are destined for something big, you should be prepared to take a leap of faith and traverse the unknown territory.

I took that leap of faith for the first time when I decided to start a business rather than pursuing higher studies. It was not a very tough choice; I knew if I had to make more money in less time, business was the way forward. Completing my studies would mean waiting for many years before becoming able to earn money. If I used that same time, I could start running the household myself and save some amount for future endeavours.

Keeping that in mind, I looked around for the business I could start. I had observed many already, and the most enticing one was that of a convenience store. This business required little investment and did not require a lot of expertise. I did not have to have elaborate English language skills to sell products at the store. And I could make good money. So, this was a good idea to start with.

So, I shared this idea with my brother one day, *"I want to do business."*

"Well, do you have any plan, any clue about what you want to do?"

"Yes, I think I should be good with running a convenience store. There's one I know of. It's going in loss. The owners are selling it for £ 3000."

"This much amount? You'd also need more money to buy the products with."

"Yes, that too. We can arrange £ 3000, but we'd need at least £ 5000 more."

"Probably then we should take a loan from the bank."

We went to the bank and got the money we needed. Now, I was in debt. With this store, I had to make enough money to not only run the household and pay all the store dues but also save enough to repay the loan. It was a heavy task, but I was more than ready to take the challenge. I had burnt my boats, and there was no retreating from this business.

I ran the convenience store for 12 long years with the help of my wife. Life went on, and we had three wonderful daughters. I saw big dreams for them. We wanted them to get a good education, find great spouses for themselves, stand on their own feet and be highly qualified, strong, independent women someday. Meanwhile, at the convenience store, the income was more or less the same. With this amount, I began to realise, we would not be able to afford our daughters the lifestyle we wanted.

I decided it was time to have a discussion with my wife.

"Mina, this convenience store thing is not going to make us rich."

"It is our bread and butter, Shashi."

"Yes, it is, but with the money it offers, we cannot fulfil our dreams for our daughters, and we cannot have a good retirement."

"I see."

"You know what, Mina? I want my daughters to have every opportunity I was denied in my youth. I also want us to enjoy our lives after retirement. We have worked so hard in our early married life. I at least want us to retire with a

lot of money in our accounts so that we can travel the world and live the best life there is."

"Okay, so what is your plan, Shashi?"

"I think it is time to take a huge jump."

"What do you mean by that?"

"Look, I think I've had enough of this store. I want to try my hands with some other business now. You'll help me, will you?"

"Of course! I've taken the oath to be by your side through thick and thin on our wedding. I'll always support you in whatever endeavour you choose to do. But what will you do?"

"Not sure. But I'll target something in the food industry. You might have to look after the store until I set up a new venture."

"Sure, honey."

We had a series of discussions on this topic. I would explore the opportunities I came across and plan things in my head. Back at home, I would discuss them with my wife.

This went on for some time until I came across the idea of opening a coffee franchise.

My reasons for joining the food industry were quite elaborate. Food was the one thing that people ate every day, many times a day. If there was one thing that had an ever-growing market, it was food. Everything else would run out of demand, but food would be there to stay. This was the time when Mc Donalds and Burger King were blossoming on all the continents of the world. Their demand was increasing with each passing day. During this time, the franchise culture was expanding like never before.

I wanted to target the fast food industry because it was much more appealing. I did not think of starting a restaurant offering different traditional food because the market for such kind of food was limited. Secondly, to make it a success, I needed to be very careful about the taste, which meant hiring professional chefs as I could not do it myself thanks to my disinterest in cooking.

Hiring somebody else for producing the major product would imply my business would be dependent on the chefs. All in all, this business model was very uncertain. I wanted to invest in one in which I did not have to rely on somebody to attract customers for me. I wanted to sell something which people needed and would therefore throng to it.

117

I was interested in franchises. Hence, I started attending franchise exhibitions. There, all kinds of the corporate elite would be there to share and sell their ideas. One of the best parts about attending such events was that I could rub shoulders with those already in the business and develop a good understanding of the way these worked. Also, they were going to help me decide which niche I should target in the vast fast food industry. I made a couple of friends who were already in the business and had lengthy chit chats with them.

It was in the year 1995 that I bumped into a coffee franchise back in Australia. The owners were planning on expanding their sales in the UK, and they needed franchisees to operate on their behalf. The idea of selling coffee was quite new at that point in time in the UK. There were not many coffee shops in here. After long hours of deliberations and discussions, I came to the conclusion that the demand for coffee could be created here with diligent efforts and the right strategy in place.

Another benefit of opening coffee shops was that it was a product for all kinds of people, no matter what their cultural or religious background may be. Unlike alcohol, coffee was a beverage that was not prohibited by any faith, so it was an excellent choice. Secondly, it had an ever-growing demand in different parts of the world. That motivated us to market it to the people of the UK. I was sure we could make many coffee lovers out there and capture the market with time.

We understood that the profit margin in this business would be low, but it didn't matter to me. I was confident that the transitions would be higher. Hence, our chances of making sales would be much higher, and we could make a lot more money due to heavy sales volume. I talked about it to my brother, who was going to be my partner and together, we jumped into the franchise world.

We spoke to their head office in Australia. We had a detailed talk with them before signing the agreement. Following that, some regular details were shared, terms of conditions were finalised, and all the legal paperwork happened quite fast. It was the year 1996 when we opened our first shop with hopes of it doing great. I looked after each and every small detail of the shop myself. I wanted to make sure everything was up to the mark and all the required arrangements were in place.

Fortunately, our first outlet just took off. People would come in hordes to buy coffee. Many of them even became our regular customers. Coffee was not very popular in England. The people of the UK did not know what cappuccino was. They wanted to give it a try and ended up falling in love with it. They found it quite novel and were super impressed with the taste.

We chose a really good location for the store near the shopping centre. It was the place where customers were already looking for nice beverages, so they would come to our shops. Soon after, the money came coming in, and I was extremely happy about the prospects of multiplying this venture. We did not abandon our convenience store for good measure. My wife was running the convenience store while my brother and I were focusing on the coffee business.

In those days, life got super busy. I would leave home early for opening the coffee shop. We had a few employees. So, we had to busy ourselves with work too. During the free time, I would often take rounds to see how the business was going and if the customers' needs were being looked after adequately. My wife, on the other hand, would get the kids ready for school, make breakfast, and after getting done with home chores, she would go to the store and run it all day long.

After a full day of work, I would meet my family at night when it was time to close the store. That was the only time I got to spend with my family. At night, I would have a light chit chat with my mother, my wife, and my three daughters.

120

As a businessman, I had to be there at my shop even on the weekends, so I lacked time to give to my family. Luckily, my family was very supportive. They never complained or opposed me in any way for not giving them enough time. They understood my work was important for our collective future.

With time, more and more money kept coming into my account. There came the point in 1998 when we did not need the convenience store at all. The money coming from coffee sales was enough to meet our expenses and make good savings for future investments as well. So, a big moment came in my life when I sold the store and moved into a new house thanks to the amount I was earning in coffee shops.

The year 1999 was a huge turning point in my career. In this very year, I had to take the most difficult decision of my life. At this time, we had three shops running with full fervour, but there was a disagreement between my brother and me as far as future plans were concerned.

My brother and I were not on the same wavelength. My brother was a pessimist, whereas I was an optimist. He was a qualified accountant who thought we should not go ahead with the franchise. If we did, we would only incur losses. My brother wanted to stop there and then. He was not a risk-taker at all. He believed the existing shops were enough and that with their help, we could live on the fat of the land in some years time.

I, on the other hand, wanted to grow faster. I knew if we kept going with this pace and that if we continued, there was no doubt we would make a lot more money than what we were making. As they say, desperate times call for desperate measures. Our disagreement was so strong that we could not seem to get along together in the future. Hence, after lots of discussions, convincing, and negotiations, it was time to take another tough decision.

I decided to discuss the matter with my family. My mother, wife, and my daughters all sat down for a positive and productive session on the future of our coffee business. By this time, my three daughters were big enough to contribute in the discussion. After a long, fruitful session, we decided that for all of us to enjoy a healthy future, we really needed to put our foot down. Luckily, my entire family shared my views and left it on me to proceed with my plans.

Parting ways with my brother was perhaps the most challenging of all the decisions I had to take in my business. I did not want to affect the bond with my brother. So, I had to tread on this path very carefully. The two of us had a nice chat, and with the agreement of both of us, we decided to go our separate ways. We ascertained that this decision would not impact our relationship in any way. My brother was contented with the decision, and he wished me luck for the future. We would continue to meet with each other and lived close together for the coming years, only our business separated.

In the year 2000, we divided our three shops between us. He got two and I one. From that point on, I put all my energy into expanding the business with franchises and began grooming myself for future endeavours. I would try every way I could to fine-tune my business. Now, I was the sole decision-maker in the business, and other people only had to follow. So, there was a huge responsibility on my shoulders. My decisions could make or break the situation. If they proved productive enough, I would get the credit; if they didn't, I would bear the cost because I was the sole owner.

As challenging as it sounds, I was actually enjoying the process. In about 2004, I opened more shops making me an owner of four shops in total. Just the next year, I had one more shop. With five shops in my ownership now, I went to the bank to seek a million-pound loan. I got the loan quite easily, and with the money I had acquired, I doubled the number of my stores. Now, I had ten fully running and profit-making stores in different locations. Our sales more than doubled, earnings doubled, and liabilities doubled. With that, the adrenaline supply in my body doubled too.

Chapter 12: Life Of An Entrepreneur

If you ask me what it means to be an entrepreneur, I'd say it does not mean any one thing. Rather it is a combination of attitudes, approaches, and mindset that makes you an entrepreneur. Being an entrepreneur is not easy, but it is not impossible either. In many ways, it boils down to the drive you have to make money and dedicate everything you have to this cause and create experiences for people. Anybody who can do that and keep going despite all the hurdles that pop up in their way can become an entrepreneur. Perhaps I am an example of how you could start from scratch and become a successful entrepreneur without any back and with hardly any money.

Right before I started working, I had two options. Either I could get a job, or I could start my own business. With the education I had, I could only get a menial labour job, which was physically hard. Also, it could not afford me the lifestyle I aimed for myself. One of the biggest benefits of having a business is that there are daily earnings and daily profits. The harder and better I worked, the higher money I could make. On the other hand, the amount of money to be made in a job was always limited according to the number of hours you worked. At the same time, however, I knew doing business would be much more stressful as there were no fixed hours, and there was also a possibility of incurring losses. But I was driven to embark on business because I knew only here could I earn huge sums of money. I was dreaming big, and business is for big dreamers.

The first step in business is often the most difficult one. It is the point where you have to commit yourself to a goal that is neither easy nor predictable. You have all the options laid bare before you. It is not as simple as it sounds. You have to have a powerful pushing factor behind your decision. Unfortunately, many people just go by the illusion they have of the business world without committing themselves to the business completely. It looks very glorified from the outside, but what they fail to see is that if you become a failure, then you can end up in a much worse position than when you started out. Hence, you should embark on a business only when you are willing to commit yourself to it.

In my case, everything was quite clear. I had seen poverty all my life before coming to the UK, and I knew that the only way I could earn respect in society was by earning a lot of money. There was no way I could make this much money except by doing business. So, I was dead confident that business was the only way to go ahead, and I committed myself to it completely before buying the convenience store. From that point on, I never looked back.

As an entrepreneur, one of the first things I learnt was public dealing. In the initial days of the convenience store, my English was quite weak. I would have difficulty understanding the customers sometimes. At other times, I had a hard time pronouncing things correctly. However, I polished my language skills in the field. There's no better way to learn something than practising it and using it for earning money.

Perhaps the strongest point that helped me a lot in the business was my childhood hardships. Whatever I had faced during my childhood, all the rejections, all the hardships, all the embarrassment I had to go through made me an extremely tough man. You have to be tough to succeed in a business. There are many points where you would experience rejections and failures. Everybody goes through such experiences, including some of the biggest businessmen today. However, the ones who succeed in the face of setbacks are those who overcome all pain, physical as well as emotional and bounce back quickly. Luckily in my case, my childhood experiences had moulded me into the kind of man who was not afraid of failures or challenges. That helped me keep going in the face of difficulties.

Struggle and challenges are part and parcel of the life of an entrepreneur. Every single day would demand sacrifices to be made along the way. So if you want to become an entrepreneur, know that you will give up on a number of dreams and aspirations of yours. As for me, I was already willing to sacrifice everything to achieve my goals. When others would be going on vacations and spending money generously, I was saving every single penny to invest in my business. When the others had scrumptious food, I was surviving on meagre munching here and there so that I could focus all my energies on making sales. That is how bit by bit, I grew my business until the time came when I could afford all the luxuries of the world.

A problem-solving approach is a prerequisite to becoming a successful entrepreneur. In business, you are dealing with a plethora of things on a daily basis, and not everything happens as per your plans. Also, not every time things would happen smoothly. So, be prepared for the challenges that come your way. Everything that hinders your money-making prospects is a challenge, and every challenge is an opportunity in disguise. It is upon you to embrace the existing challenges and find solutions to them.

In my case, with time, I got so used to finding solutions to problems that they stopped bothering me. A point came when I loved looking at challenges in the eye and finding efficient solutions to them. Whenever a problem case, I would never say, *"Oh No, Here's another one"*. Rather I would say, *"Here's another challenge. Let's embrace it. Let's begin the fun."* Here's a takeaway for you – learn to enjoy the process of finding solutions rather than getting afraid of the problem or fearing the consequences if anything went wrong. The more you enjoy it, the better you will perform at it.

As a businessman, I had my priorities defined beforehand. I had already planned on saving each and every penny and sacrifice my ease and comfort for this purpose. So, in the first six months of running the convenience store, I had a cardboard box placed behind the sofa. When it was time to shut down the store, I would drag it out and sleep on it for the night. It was definitely not a comfortable experience, but I did not care about comfort. I did not have surplus money to buy a bed; it was not my priority either. I knew my initial days would be struggling, but I also knew that if I kept going like that, I would definitely enjoy comfort some time down the line.

One of the most commonplace things in a business is risk-taking. The very first decision of pursuing business as a career carries risk. As you go along, you come across many events where you have to make a tough choice, and you have to risk your money. When I first invested in the convenience store, I had taken loan from the bank as well as from my friends. If it did not turn out well, where would I return the money from? Similarly, when I was expanding, I took a million-pound loan from the bank. If things turned sour, I'd have to let go of my assets. There is risk involved in each and every step in the life of an entrepreneur. But it is the same risk that makes doing business all the more thrilling. Where you can incur a loss, you can also make huge profits if you work on your strategy and learn from your experiences.

One of the biggest enemies of your success is fear. A lot of people miss great opportunities due to fear. They fear many unfounded fears such as the fear of failure, challenges, rejection from society, etc. However, one thing which I have learnt in my journey is that you have to control your apprehensions and not let them control you. When your attitudes and thinking are on the right track, you don't have to be fearful of anything or anybody. Let me give you examples from my life. I did not fear failure because I knew every failure had some valuable lessons for me. I did not fear people because I did not care about them. And I did not fear challenges because I found them exciting. So, the key lesson to eliminate fear from the equation is to change your thinking pattern and approach towards things.

When I was growing my business, my mind was always occupied. I kept thinking about money and prospects. In my head, I would be making calculations all the time. As an entrepreneur, your brain never switches off. You have to think on behalf of everybody else because it is your money that is at stake. When I was expanding, I had to be very careful about putting a system in place which would function in the most efficient manner. When my shops were dispersed here and there, I had to survey them and note the complaints or suggestions of the people so that I could improve the system better.

When my workload increased, I started looking after my health better. I would wake up early, exercise daily to keep myself fit and healthy. Some people ignore their health while focusing all their attention on business, but I, for one, would never encourage that. Nothing is worthwhile when your health is not in the right state. In fact, when you are healthy, you can perform better at all the tasks awaiting you. Eating healthy and exercising daily proved extremely beneficial for me. It would make me ready for the next day and also provide me with a sharp focus and better memory.

An entrepreneur should always have a learning attitude. They rightly say a winning attitude is a learning attitude. I would learn from everybody, the clients, my employees, and whoever I realised could teach me something valuable. If I saw my employees doing something differently or if I realised they knew better about some issue, I was always open to learning from them. That way, I kept becoming a better businessman and a better learner with every passing day.

Businessmen face new problems every single day. Problems always arise in businesses. To overcome them, you have to react positively. On my part, however, whenever an anomaly came up, I would break it down into small pieces to find its origin. I would join the dots, 'this happened because of that decision', 'this is linked to our new product', etc., to find the cause. So, by doing that, I would reach a couple of conclusions such as 'Maybe we aren't marketing ourselves enough', 'maybe we can accelerate the process', etc. In this way, I would discuss things with the other stakeholders and even my staff at times to get to the roots of the issue and deal with it head-on.

One of the most important qualities of successful businessmen is that they look after their employees. For me, my employees were like a family. I would actively engage myself in solving their problems. Keep this in mind; they cannot work if they are worried or if they have something bothering them all the time. So, I would investigate and interrogate them if I found them disturbed. When they were happy and healthy, they performed to the best of their abilities, and that only helped my business grow with leaps and bounds.

When you plan to do business, keep in mind that you'd have to work hard day and night, and perhaps you may not get to take a rest for days. For example, when I had multiple stores, my job also became tougher. I had to answer multiple people, solve many problems at a time, manage humans, attend meetings, look after the legalities, etc. All this required a great deal of time and effort on my part. I could choose to sit at home and rely on other people to look after my business, but that could be damaging for my business in the long run. So, I took it upon myself to oversee my business regularly.

Being an entrepreneur means you are not entitled to any vacations, holidays or off days, especially during the formative phase of your business. Whatever happens to you on the personal level, whatever problems you face at home should not deter you from showing up on the business. There were times in my life, too, when someone in my family was ill, or there was some problem bothering all of us, but I would not take off days just like that. I would be there in the shop the very next day because my customers were expecting me to be there and because I was known for my punctuality. I would not just go there and sit. In fact, I would also have to make sure my mind was present and active while carrying out the business so that the level of trust I had with my customers did not falter.

As an entrepreneur, your attitude is very important. You have to remain calm and humble. You treat people with respect; you earn respect in return. Some people change their attitude, get a little harsh, and assume airs, but that is a damaging approach. What they end up doing is losing the support of their customers or even their employees when bad days hit. I never made that mistake, and that is why I enjoyed a lot of support from my clients and my employees in all the endeavours I picked up.

Once I was in this line, I knew there was no going back. Slowly and gradually, I kept building on my business with little improvements I could make to the store and then to the coffee shops later. I was assured I was heading in the right direction because I was going at my pace. I did not make a haphazard decision to become an overnight millionaire or made a foolish investment, for that matter. I was going step by step because every step leads you to a higher step. You could not make a huge jump and expect to be landed on the top. You may just fall face down on the ground.

After doing business for many years, I also provided coaching to others. It gives me immense satisfaction to help others build their businesses. It is also one of the ways of giving back to society. I teach the aspiring entrepreneurs the lessons I had learned the hard way so that they could capitalise on my mistakes and circumvent them in their journey. When I make somebody stand on their own two feet, I feel successful.

Chapter 13: Fatherhood

I still remember the first time I became a father. It was one of the nights of 1986. Mina had been in labour for 24 hours. I was desperately walking around the corridor while my mother kept praying to God for a healthy child. I closed my eyes, and images from the last nine months played in front of me just like the scenes of a movie.

The day we received the news of Mina's pregnancy. The smile that braced my mother's heavenly face at the thought of becoming a grandmother. The nights when we slept, thinking about how our lives would change with the child. The times when I was working extra hard at the convenience store because I had promised to give my child the best possible future. All the ups and downs we had during Mina's pregnancy. Everything just became live until I heard the shrieking sound of a newborn.

"Congratulations, Mr Shashi. You became a father to a beautiful girl", the nurse announced as she exited the delivery room, hinting me to get in and meet my firstborn. I had goosebumps as I heard the news. I remember the entire scene as if it just happened yesterday. Mina was holding our first child. She smiled at me, handing over my baby girl in my arms carefully. Looking at her, I realised, *"It was worth the hardship"*.

Holding your child is perhaps the best feeling in the whole wide world. I could not get over the softness of her skin. The red, goofy baby laid in my arms as though she knew she would be protected here. She opened her big eyes and looked at her 'daddy'. She smelled so nice I couldn't get over holding her in my arms. *"Our prayers had been answered. We became parents, Mina"*. We both looked at the baby and smiled.

Our marriage was three years old when he had our first daughter. Becoming parents wasn't as difficult as raising the child combined with running a store. Soon after my first daughter was born, I took leave from my wife and mother as I had to run the store and bring in money. Our family was expanding now. As happy as we were with the arrival of our first child, we could not forget we had more mouths to feed now and hence the sense of responsibility towards work doubled.

A couple of days after the delivery, Mina joined me at the convenience store. She said she had taken enough rest and that it was time to work hard, so we provide our child with everything she deserved. Unlike today where mothers are advised to look after their health and take rest all day long, my wife chose to forget her comfort for the future of our child. Her sense of duty and perseverance kindled new energy in me. At that moment, I knew my daughter had many role models to look up to in her life.

Mina would take small breaks from store work to look after the baby. She would feed her, dress her up and put her to sleep. When she wasn't available, my mother would look after the baby. We'd make sure her work schedule did not interfere with the baby's needs. So, Mina would take leave early to do home chores and spend quality time with the baby. I, on the other hand, would stay at the store and work till night. This, after all, was the bread and butter for our growing family.

After a long, tiring day at work, I looked forward to holding my daughter and hugging her tight. My daughter received me with a smile as she began to realise I was her 'dad'. Her touch was the most magical thing in the world. The moment I took her in your arms, all my tiredness went away. My daughter was a healthy baby, and she grew bubblier with time. Holding her and caressing her was a mighty blessing.

Some of the fondest memories I have of life involve me playing with my daughter and not getting enough of it. She was the most beautiful thing that had ever happened to us. Perhaps I was not this happy at my marriage even. As new parents, we had to learn a number of things for the first time, such as burping the child, putting the right ratio of water and milk in the bottle, ensuring the feeder was mildly hot, changing the diapers, and helping the child with gastric problems. Thankfully, we had my mother to train us in these areas. We never had any difficulty in terms of handling the baby. Every time there was a problem beyond the scope of our understanding, Mina and I would go straight to my mother, and she'd come up with ways to relieve the child.

Our first daughter was only two years old when we had a second one. Born in 1988, our second child was born with a smile on her face, unlike other children who cry their lungs out as soon as they enter the world. Our daughter, born in the summers of July, was as bright and warm as the month of her arrival. She announced her arrival with a wide smile.

Back at home, our family grew bigger. We made space for another daughter in the room. There were toys all around the house. Our most go to shops were those selling kids' stuff. Our most-watched shows were the cartoons my daughters liked to watch. And so, everything began to take shape as per the needs and wants of our daughters. Our lifestyle began to be defined by them.

Our two daughters had a very small age difference between them, but as hard as it sounds, raising two kids, both small, was actually a blessing in disguise. Our two daughters gelled in really well from a very young age. As infants, they were like two little buddies trying to understand each other. They devised a language of their own. We'd often see them smiling at each other as if they were developing a warm, sisterly love. The two of them were like companions with a strong bond of affection between them.

Now I had two angels to embrace me and take all my stress away after reaching home. I cannot forget how they would come running to me when I stepped inside the home, each trying to give her father the tightest hug. I would take them both in my arms and lift them up. They meant the world to me. However, having children also meant lots of sleepless nights. There were times when one of them or both would get ill or have stomach aches bothering them. We would stay up all night and calm them down. Sometimes, I would take them in my arms and walk around till they slept on my shoulders.

Back at the convenience store, I noticed I was growing more conscious of time. I knew how important an asset time was. We can get everything back except time. As my daughters were growing up fast, their father was also growing in his own way. I was becoming more confident in myself. I knew the importance of doing things at the right time. In my decision making, I was getting firmer. I somehow realised now that standing by your decisions was as crucial as taking them in the first place. As I look at it today, I believe I was growing as an entrepreneur in the true sense of the word, and a lot of the credit for that change goes to my daughters.

Life was beautiful with two angels, and soon after, we were blessed for the third time with our youngest daughter. Our home filled with joy once again, and we were again celebrating the arrival of our final baby. Our youngest one was a very smart looking and cute child. She had two oldest sisters, a loving mother, and an experienced grandmother to guide her through different times. There's no doubt she was very lucky to have amazing ladies around.

All three of our daughters got their looks from Mina. They were super gorgeous like her. All of them had jet black hair, a small pointed nose, big brown eyes and a thin frame like their mother. They were going to be attractive ladies in the future like their mother, I knew for sure. And it proved true. As they became bigger, they looked like three different versions of their mother. However, they got their brains from their father.

All my daughters were brilliant in mathematics like me. They would solve any problem in no time, and I couldn't help being proud of them. With time, it was further revealed that they possessed strong decision making and problem-solving skills. They were going to be boss ladies in the future. They led by their head. You could put them in a situation, and rest assured they'd carve a way out thanks to their critical thinking skills.

My girls often say, *"we're daddy's girls"*. I cannot explain the pride they have on their face while saying that. They are extremely happy to have a hard-working, self-made father and want to follow my steps in their professional life and those of their mother in the personal sphere. I have always tried to give the best life ever to my daughters. Everything I was denied in my childhood, I made sure my daughters were not, and that paid off eventually.

Needless to say, guaranteeing my daughters a wealthy life would mean working hard day in and out. That meant I got little time to spend with them and to take them to recreation. There were days when it felt super hard to leave my girls early and come back to find them sleeping for consecutive days. But every time I looked at their innocent faces, a voice inside my head said, *"Shashi, you have to promise them a prosperous future."*

Just then, I would find myself working harder and without any regrets. I was at peace on the inside because I imagined my daughters getting a college degree, making a successful career out of it, and enjoying their life in the best manner possible. I started getting the fruits of my dedication to work when I saw them acing every field of life. Every small achievement of theirs reminded me, *"Shashi, you're on the right track. Keep going like it. Your hard work is brightening your children's future."* With that, I'd pat on my shoulder and keep going.

It was our conscious decision to complete our family fast so that we could get done with producing children and focus on raising them. We decided together that we would complete our family first, and then we would pay attention to work so that we nurture our children in a healthy environment. Also, having children with small gaps was not a bad idea. This way, our daughters learned from each other. That actually saved us a lot of time and effort since the girls were always engaged in something together and learned from each other.

My first one was extremely dedicated to her work and studies. She was good at school. Her discipline from a very young age was exemplary. Thanks to her, the rest of the two girls, too, grew up to be disciplined and hard-working. When the oldest one started going to school at the age of three, she looked all the cuter in colourful dresses with matching bands and clips. Seeing her, the other two wanted to go to school too. They followed their eldest sister in everything. That's how sisters are, I guess.

Life has been kind to me in that it gave me enough time to live some moments of eternal joy with my girls. I cannot forget the times when Christmas was around the corner. My little girls would write notes to Santa to send in their toys and gifts. We would stay up all night, rapping their gifts, hiding them from the girls, and acting as if Santa left those for them. The happiness of my girls upon seeing the gifts was worth an entire night spent preparing them.

Similarly, on events like mother's day and father's day, my girls would surprise us with handmade cards and cakes when they grew older. They would plan our special days ahead and find ways to make us feel special. To this day, we have saved the tokens of love we received from their tiny hands. Reading the cards they made in their childish handwriting makes me feel as if it was just yesterday when I picked them up in my arms and kissed their soft cheeks.

When I was a child, it was considered almost a matter of survival to have a male heir. People in India, for the most part, would go to all lengths to have a male child. There are various reasons for that, such as a male child carries the name of the family forward, is a source of earning, looks after the parents in their old age, etc. In my case, however,

I'm happy to say that not having a son never bothered me. My mother even said I should have a son too, but I explained to her I could live with pride and happiness even without one.

The problem with the desired gender is that you could go on and producing children and end up not raising them well due to time and resource constraints. What was important to me was to be the best father to my children and make them productive, independent human beings. As far as having three daughters was concerned, I was ecstatic with my girls. They are the brightness in our life. There is nothing a son could do that my daughters cannot.

My girls are strong, educated, and cultured women today. They are good enough to lead happy, healthy, and successful life. They don't depend on anybody to look after them or to support them. They keep vising us frequently. They've given us wonderful grandchildren with whom we love to spend our time. Even though they are all married today and have their own families, my daughters still take good care of their mom and me.

With every new child, my relationship with Mina got stronger. We would play our parts in raising the girls in a healthy way. When the girls received prizes in the community hall school or when they took their first step or when they performed well at sports, our chests filled with pride. We are so happy to have three beautiful daughters that we don't wish for anything else.

Looking back through the pages of the past, I feel time passed way too fast. If I were asked to relive some part of my life, I would go back in time and enjoy life with my small daughters once again.

Here are some pictures from my girls childhood and our early parenthood.

147

Chapter 14: Raising A Family

Born in a small in Indian Gujrat, I was the youngest of three brothers. We had no sister. I didn't even know what it was like to have a sister. I had no clue how to behave with girls, what to tell them, what not to teach them, what are their likes and dislikes, etc. And God chose me to raise three beautiful daughters and raise them to make me highly proud one day. They were indeed a blessing to me.

I cannot forget the moments of mirth and joy we experienced when the girls were small. My daughters' laughter brightened my life, and I wished the best of everything for them. I would tell my wife, *"Mina, our daughters will be educated, cultured ladies when they grow up."* And Mina would respond, *"I have no doubt about that, Shashi."* We dreamt of a life full of success and contentment for our daughters, and they did fulfil our dreams.

Raising three kids one after the other was not an easy task. Thankfully, my wife, who had two sisters, was well versed in the art of dealing with girls. We also had the expertise of my mother to look up to. These two women played a significant role in the wholesome upbringing of my daughters. They would teach the girls every small thing, focus on their manners, teach them our values, look after their health, and keep their eyes on them.

We had a very different environment at home. Our everyday communications would be a mix of Gujarati, Hindi, and English. My mother, for instance, would talk to my girls in Gujarati, and my daughters would respond in English initially. The communication between the two was often hilarious. However, the best part was they understood each other despite the language gap. At home, the women of the house provided an environment filled with cultural and religious values for the girls to stay connected to their roots.

My wife and mother inculcated our Indian values in my girls very nicely. They would tell them stories about our background and teach our traditional values to them. From a very young age, my daughter knew they had to pay respect to the elders and treat others well. They knew they had to be kind to others. These are the things they absorbed by looking at their mother and grandmother. They were not only cognizant of our values, but they also made them a part of their behaviour.

We made sure our daughters were well aware of the Indian traditional festivals. To ensure that, we took them to gatherings for *Holi*, *Diwali*, and *Navratri*. My daughters would learn the *Garba*, a traditional dance we perform at *Navratri*. Our culture and festivals are so rich that my daughters were automatically drawn towards them. It is not

149

easy to do the *Garba*. It requires hours and hours of practice, but my girls kill it because they have learned it out of interest and not out of compulsion.

Although the Indian culture was important for my daughters, English culture was more so. After all, they were supposed to live here all their lives, and they would be raising their kids in the same culture. So, at school, we ensure their active participation in events like Christmas plays, Duke of Edinburgh awards, and other traditional Western activities.

I always think in a mathematical way. Most of my decisions come from the brain and not the heart. My girls' upbringing was done rationally from my end. I was very clear about where they should spend their time and what they should avoid. For example, they spoke reasonably good Gujrati with my mother, but I never forced it on them. The thing with Gujrati is that it is a complex language, not simple like English. And aside from my mother, there was no one they would converse in Gujrati with, so there was no point making them work hard in learning it. The same energy could be better utilised at a more productive job.

When my daughters were small, I told my wife, *"Mina, don't call them into the kitchen."* She would ask, *"But they will have to learn to cook eventually?"* *"Well, they will when the time comes. At this point, what matters the most is their education. Let them focus on that. There should be no distraction in their way right now."* I explained to Mina, *"Look, Mina. Here's the deal. If our daughters are educated enough, they'll hire somebody to do the home chores with sufficient finances. But if they don't have a good education, they'll have to work extra hard only to survive, and there's no way they could afford a better lifestyle without education".*

I was very clear about education. You have a good degree, your chances of landing a good position and leading a wealthy life brighten. You may not become a millionaire with your education, but you will have a good enough job and would not have to grind yourself to make both ends meet. You can lead a life of dignity with a handsome income flowing into your account every month. You would not have to take favours from anyone.

With these views, I wanted my girls to get a damn good degree and make a career first and foremost. Everything else came later. When my first daughter was small, I started looking for schools for her. When she reached three, I got her admitted to a private school. Those who are familiar with the education system in the UK know how grossly expensive private schools are. So, it wasn't easy to finance their education. We saved from everywhere just so we could support our daughters' education.

I could have chosen a government school for my girls, but the businessman inside me said, *"Education is a service. You're paying for it, you can demand a good service. The higher you pay, the better service you'd get. Go for a private school, Shashi"*. And there I was. Since I wanted to give my daughters everything in time, I picked a private school for their education.

Being a time-conscious man, I understood how crucial it was to have an excellent start to one's academic life. Education cannot be acquired at the age of fifty or sixty for the most part. It has an age limit. So, I had to be very cautious about every step in the academic life of my daughters. I could not make a decision, only to regret it ten years later. In a small time frame, I had to choose between good and best, and I chose the best for my girls.

Time passed so quickly that it seemed only yesterday when my eldest daughter was going to complete her GCSE. Being the first one in the family to do that, it was big news for our relatives and us. I couldn't pursue higher studies in the UK because I had more pressing things to do. But I made sure my girls got higher education. With her hard work and our efforts, my eldest daughter got admission to Cambridge after her A levels. Her brilliant mind and unflinching determination paved her way to Cambridge and behind her was the staggering support of her parents, who had worked super hard to support their daughter's education.

Having a daughter going to one of the most prestigious universities in the world was a dream come true. The dream I saw when my firstborn was in my arms. She internalised our aspirations into hers and made them come true. Soon after, our respect in the community increased manifold. People now recognised the struggles of an uneducated man who had learned through the hard experiences of life, built an empire, and sent his children to the most prestigious institutes of the world.

If you remember, I talked about a hard decision of parting ways with my brother and operating my coffee business separately. I also discussed I took the decision because, without expansion, we would not be able to provide the standard life to my girls. Now, my decisions and my struggles were paying off. I also sent my eldest daughter to pursue a Master's degree in the USA for one year, and there too, she continued making us proud.

In the meantime, my second daughter cleared her GCSE and then A-levels. She also landed in one of the renowned varsities in the UK, the Universities of Warwick. My other two daughters had it easy. They had a leader in the form of their eldest sibling. She set the standard very high and guided her sisters to achieve it. She had been a leader since a very young age. My other two girls saw her determination, her efforts, and smartness, and they followed in her footsteps from the very beginning.

My third daughter, too, continued the trend and landed in King's College. It was like a formality now. One after the other, my daughters achieved the milestones we had set for them in their academic life. All three of them made their parents immensely proud. Not only did they get the best education, but they did it in due time. I wanted them to wrap up their degrees in one go, without any gaps, and they did just that. By the age of 23 or 24, my girls had a Bachelor's degree and were capable of making a future for themselves.

I didn't have a higher education degree, but life provided me with ample exposure to groom myself and have an objective outlook of the world. I used the same exposure and lessons derived from my experiences in the corporate world to guide my daughters. In the business world, I had seen and met enough people to be able to teach my family the right approach to life matters. That proved very fruitful for my girls too.

From the very beginning, I wanted my daughters to be street smart. Only bookish knowledge would not suffice to survive and succeed in this world. There was a desperate need to develop their social and interpersonal skills. Those were the things schools didn't train their pupils for, so I took it upon myself to teach them to my girls.

I would explain the lessons I had learned in life the hard way to my daughters. We would discuss business and entrepreneurship. We talked about survival without any external help. We deliberated upon the importance of becoming so self-sufficient that you did not have to seek any kind of help. I often shared examples from my life in Kaliari to teach some important lessons to my daughters.

My girls were very smart. They had seen our struggles, and they knew what it took to start from absolutely nothing and build an empire by only relying on yourself, your skills, and your hard work. My daughters would ask me questions about my life and what I did in different situations. They were clearly taking mental notes and learning from second-hand experiences. They were also very empathetic. When they were small, both Mina and I had a tight schedule at work. Sometimes, we'd come late. There were times when we weren't able to give a lot of time to them. I was lucky that my daughters understood why mommy and daddy had to do all of that. They knew it was for their good that we worked hard at the store. They never made a fuss about it. Rather, they were always supportive and encouraging.

The home life of my girls was taken care of mostly by my wife and my mother. My role, on the other hand, was more active in their education. I would make sure they were doing their schoolwork right, paying attention to studies, taking part in academic and co-curricular activities, and performing well in them. Some of the proudest moments from their childhood are them winning prizes, earning certificates, and trophies for stellar performance. Even to this day, we have their medals and awards decorated in our homes. We still see them receiving their awards in pictures and smile.

I always wanted my girls to have well-rounded personalities. That is why I encouraged them to participate in sports too. My daughters were pretty good at karate, tennis, and a variety of sports. They got a reasonable taste of fun and enjoyment in the form of sports. We still talk to them about their school days and recall the times they used to win prizes at sports. It was such fun seeing my daughters acing them.

When my daughters were in their early teens, I involved them in important decisions. I believe their say was very important and that they should have the ability to make decisions from a very young age. When I decided to separate my coffee business from my brother, my daughters stood by my decision. They had an understanding of the kind of work we did and what entrepreneurship really meant. I think involving kids in critical decisions is essential for their growth and maturity. Only that way, you could enable them to be independent thinkers, planners, and decision-makers.

Where business had occupied an important place in my life, parenting was much more crucial a task than business. In business, you always have another chance if something goes wrong. People face bankruptcies and start all over again. But the same is not guaranteed in parenting. If you didn't raise your kids right in the first place, you cannot go back in time and start afresh. Hence, parenting was a much more serious business. I made sure I put my heart and soul into it and get it right.

As time passed, my daughters stood on their own two feet and were able to find the right partners for themselves. Being a dutiful father, it was now my job to do everything my daughters desired for their wedding. I asked them what they wanted for their wedding and made sure everything they asked for was done. Since they had given me everything

I wanted from them, it was time I fulfilled my promise by getting them married off in the way they dreamed of.

Life has a strange way of giving back. When I was getting married, we barely had enough money to invite more than 25 close relatives of ours. Fast forward to my daughters' weddings. I had all the resources to make sure they had a dream wedding. There were loads of guests. Everything was top-notch. We gave expensive gifts, got the best clothes made for us, and enjoyed ourselves to the core.

Surely, *"hard work pays off, and it pays off in the best manner possible"*. Today, I look at my daughters raising their kids the way we raised them and feel proud of my wife and myself. All our efforts paid off, and today we enjoy the best life with my daughters and their children. Luckily, we see our life lessons being passed on to the other generation and cannot help being grateful.

Here are some pictures of the ladies of my family.

Chapter 15: Franchise

When I held my firstborn in my hands, I had decided, *"I would give the best of everything to my child."* When I said everything, I meant the best upbringing, the best education, and the best lifestyle. While my daughter was taking her first steps, I was imagining her donning the school uniform of one of the best schools and bringing prizes home. I dreamt that she would make all of us proud one day with her academic achievements. But that would need a good base to start with.

I have always believed that children perform really well in their schools and colleges when they get the right guidance and support in the very beginning. While in their initial years, children are like a sponge. They absorb things happening around them. They take notice of our language, our behaviours, and events taking place in their surroundings quite intently. Most of that knowledge serves as the basis of children's psyche. They learn everything from their environment.

It is advisable to nurture babies in a healthy environment because they do what they see. When they start learning things actively, it is important for them to be surrounded by learned people who guide them right. I never got the chance to live with highly qualified or super smart people. Perhaps that is why I was not in a strong position academically when

I came here. Hence, I was left with two options. I could either start my education from way behind and spend a good ten years or so to earn a college degree. Else, I could get my feet wet in the business world and start making money already.

The best option for me was the latter. While I was embarking on this journey, I had already made up my mind to never let my next generation go through the same. As much as I love business, I don't want to discredit education. In my view, education makes you more civilised and provides meaningful and respectable ways of earning to you. For these reasons, it is definitely worth it. I, for one, wanted my children to be highly educated and qualified so they could make a respectable living for themselves.

One of the first things I started to do as a new father was looking for schools. I would ask people I met about different schools in the area and how they groomed the kids. There were majorly two kinds of schools; public and private. I had already explained the reasons of putting my daughters into a private school. Now, let's talk about the problem, which was the fee. It was exorbitant, to say the least.

For a person running a convenience store, affording private education for three daughters was a bit of an ordeal. And this was just the school fee. There were other expenses too – their stationaty, books, uniform, accessories, etc. Not just that, I had promised to run the house, save for our vacations, enjoy our life, and have a peaceful retirement. *"Where on earth would the money to meet my expenses come from?"* was the question that started bothering me more often than not.

This was the time when Mina and I were working 14 hours a day. Yes, we were making a reasonable amount of money, but that would not suffice when the girls grew up. With time, our expenses were only going to increase. With the money coming from the convenience store, we would have to cut down our expenses, goals in other words, and live a moderate life rather than a wealthy life. But no, I didn't even consider this possibility. All I knew was that I had to expand my income by hook or by crook and give my daughters the life I could only dream of at their age.

Around this time, the business models were changing fast all across the world. Franchises were the new mania in the business world. They were growing everywhere. We had McDonald's and KFC franchises spread all across the UK. There was a frenzy surrounding the franchise business. Many people wanted to try their hands with one or the other. I somehow felt this was where I wanted to invest my money and make higher profits. But the problem was I knew very little, and there wasn't much information readily available on them as it was a new phenomenon.

So, I started learning about franchises through whatever source I could get my hands on. I'd read magazines, interview people who had some knowledge of them. Every time I bumped into somebody who knew a great deal about franchises, I had my questions ready. As we spoke, I noted down their arguments and ideas for use in future. My mind was giving birth to new ideas.

Back in the day, research was a hundred times more laborious. There was no internet or cellular phones. At best, we could make calls and talk to people on the other end of the landline in hopes of exacting useful information out of them. Hence, my research went on for about five to six years. A routine part of this phase was attending franchise exhibitions taking place in the UK.

Exhibitions were the place where multiple franchise owners and companies would come and talk about their business models. Sometimes, it was useful; sometimes, it wasn't. Nevertheless, I never gave up on my search. It was our routine to go there and learn who came this time, what they were bringing to the UK, and if anybody had made in growth in Uk markets. It was always rewarding to learn if anybody had been achieving their profit targets in the franchise business, etc. Such information helped us analyse the situation and predict the growth prospects of the franchises.

Years of research and exposure told me that I'd need ample guidance, support, and experience on my hands to become successful in the franchise business. Those things should be able to give me a good start. Now, it was time to analyse my profile. I had no business background. I was a farmer's son. When I came here first, I barely spoke English and had no money in my pockets. Everything was against me, but I had made my way into the retail business successfully. I learned what it took and gave it my hundred per cent. That made one thing clear to me. If I had what is required to run a business and I was also willing to do what it took, there was no reason why I would fail.

The best thing about franchises was that they could enable me to achieve my financial goals much quicker. A convenience store, if you had been running it for about five to seven years, could give you a comfortable life for sure. It would, however, not allow you to make ten times more money than what you were already making. There was a tight margin in which you would make money. Not a lot higher, not much lower than that.

On the other hand, one of the most significant negatives about this business was that the risk factor was much higher. The general rule is: either you'd make a lot of money if your franchise works, or you lose your investment entirely if your model does not work sufficiently well in the market. So, all in all, this was going to be a much thrilling and risky endeavour than running a convenience store.

You had to be very cautious while entering the franchise business in those times. Back then, many people were trying to make an ingress in the market but no one had actually made it there. There were new boys on the block. The scary thing was they were only trying to experiment with the business to see how things went. But for us, who wanted to multiple our income many times, that approach only meant playing with our money. We could not take up such an endeavour just for the sake of providing data for their experiment. So, we had to tread along carefully.

On one of the days of meeting new businesses looking for promising franchisees, we came across an Australian coffee company. Theirs was a model that really intrigued us, and we soon found ourselves engaging with them more frequently for a prospective business deal. The more we studied about them, the more interested we got in their idea. Because we liked it so much, we were willing to put our heart and soul into it. Luckily for us, the Australian company was also looking for dedicated people to run the franchise in the UK. They were very nice people to work with.

They told us they had got a large number of shops in Australia and New Zealand. In one of the meetings with them, they revealed how they wanted us to get deeply acquainted with their business model. For that reason, they offered us to visit their shops and offices in the two states at their own expense. That was a rich learning experience for my brother and me. Without giving it a second thought, we left for Australia. There, we spoke to a lot of franchisees and master franchisees, learned about their experience, the way they functioned and observed their operations for a good number of days.

We would be at the franchises from morning till evening. We surveyed how they worked. Little little things helped make my mind that this was the business for me. Being a retailer, I was doing my calculations in my head already, *"two dozens of this make this", "Here, I could make a hundred pounds in profit", "This is how we can store the stock", "That's what becomes of the remaining items".* After a few days of doing these calculations, there I was, convinced that this business was definitely what I could do with utmost passion and dedication.

The reason I was interested in franchises was that they gave you the opportunity to step into a busy place, such as a shopping mall. The thing with big places like malls is that they don't entertain small companies or start-ups. I knew we just needed the name of a renowned company to put our feet in the shopping centres. Once that was done, we could easily capitalise on operations, which was our strong point. The retail business had taught us exactly how to manage stock, how to rotate it, what to order, what not to order, etc. That knowledge put us ahead in the game.

Immediately after the survey, we thought about finalising the deal on paper. All the official work happened in a matter of few days. Soon after, we started looking for sites that could bring us good business. Needless to say, our eyes were hovering over the shopping centres and surrounding areas for starting our first shop. Those were the places where people came with the intention to spend money. It was there that we could find customers who would be willing to spend a couple of bucks on a cup of coffee.

The struggle of a couple of weeks came to a positive end when we finally landed a promising place to open the first shop at. We opened our first shop in 1995. My brother and I were super excited about it. Recall that this year 1995 marked the rise and bloom of shopping malls. So, there we were, offering coffee for tired of shopping coffee lovers.

We hired a bunch of staff for our first store in 1995. Fortunately, it took off quite well despite that we were the new boys in the business. One thing we did differently from other franchises was that we focused on hiring middle-aged people. I thought the interaction between a customer and the staff member should build trust, and that could be ensured when the employee looked experienced and serious about work. Perhaps an 18-year-old boy behind the counter would not be able to make as effective an encounter.

Ours was a new concept. We needed to get everything right because we were operators in the business. Our decision helped us build a good team of serious and diligent people who were as excited as we were. I personally believe sharing your vision with the team and getting them involved in the process towards achieving the targets is very crucial. It helps them own the place and provide the best of their service.

On my part, I did not play the distant owner of the coffee shop, but I constantly engaged the employees. They were like a family to me and what I did to get them on board was that I discussed my aims and aspirations with them. I told them straight that we wanted to expand. In my pep talks to my staff, I would clearly tell them that *"We want to expand our presence across the city." "We'd all work diligently so that we could multiply our branches"*.

As I spoke to them, I could see hope for higher earning prospects in their eyes too. My growth was not only mine; it was my employees' too. They had enough confidence in my leadership that they knew if they performed well, they would advance in their career. So, it was in their good interest to boost the sales and expand the business.

Those were good times when a cup of coffee and a muffin cost three pounds. We made many sales a day and each sale got us a small profit. From 8 in the morning to late at night, people would come thronging to our shop for grabbing a cup of coffee and relaxing for a while. It was a wonderful sight. Our shop would always be full of customers to the point that there were queues. I remember walking around the shop and looking after all the matters.

Those were the times when I was working super hard to get the shop running. I would see if the quantities of ingredients were enough. I would be directing my staff members to ration the stuff beforehand. Then, I would make sure the quality is top-notch, and we were not compromising on the taste. Apart from that, I'd give special attention to cleanliness. At sharp eight in the morning, we would be ready to open the store and start selling. It became a routine for me. From early morning to late at night, I would be working at the store.

Business is built brick by brick. In the morning, especially, you have to be completely invested in it. Only then you make it work. In my case, too, it took a lot of time to build our goodwill. But it eventually paid off. People started to notice us. As time passed, we were not just a coffee franchise in the corner of a large shopping complex. We begin to earn a name for ourselves.

Here are some pictures from the early days of franchising,.

Chapter 16: Coffee

I started the coffee franchise business in 1995 and expanded it to the level that it made me a millionaire. Somebody reading this chapter at this time might think, *"This man must have been lucky to have entered the coffee business and aced it. I mean, the market is so competitive."* That's right. The market is competitive these days, but it was not when I got my feet wet with it. And the part about me being lucky needs special discussion.

As for my being lucky is concerned, perhaps I was, but more than that, I was super hard working. In the wise words of the great American President Thomas Jefferson, *"I find that the harder I work, the more luck I seem to have"*. I can vouch for this statement. The more effort you put into something, the more you know about it, and the better you perform at it. I did the same. I put in my one hundred per cent, and that got me on the right track, one where I made high profits and sustained them.

People who ask me if they should jump into the coffee business are usually the ones who are not very certain if they would succeed at it. My advice to them as well as to my reader is, *"This business is for anybody who is willing to put in the hard work"*. I'd recommend anybody to go into business provided they make a full-proof plan, implement it in letter and spirit and are willing to cater to the demands of the cunsumers even if that means making significant shifts in their ways.

As for the question, *"Are there still profits to be made in the coffee business?"* Well, yes. In our times, a cup of coffee sold for pound two and a half. Today, you can sell it for a much higher price. That shows the profit margins have only increased over time. Further, you can bring innovations to your business. So, you don't just have to sell plain coffee; you can think about trying different versions of it or add novel snacks to the menu. Also, work on the packaging and building relationships with your customers by upholding the values they stand by.

There are people who choose eco-friendly packaging for the customers. In that way, they touch the hearts of the consumers. Others offer charity to the underprivileged and thereby build a positive image of their brand. As you already know, this is not the time when you would enter the market and blow it off with a basic business model because of the level of competitiveness that prevails. But still, you can penetrate the market with a modified approach. Add value to your product, and your product will bring business to your doors.

Around the time we entered the market, it was not very competitive. That was the point when Mc Donalds and KFC were entering the UK. Business persons were trying their hands with the franchises. They would hire a small staff and open up a franchise. Now, these people would be playing on the investor's money. If it worked, good for all of them. If it didn't, the investor would bear the loss. So, it was a pretty dicey situation overall.

In my case, there was no chance of leaving the affairs of business on a handful of staff members. The reason for me entering the franchise business, as I've already told previously, was to play on a higher field. My aim was to make a lot of money and live the lifestyle of my dreams. If you remember, I was already running a convenience store at this point in time. So I was already making good money, but I wanted higher numbers. Hence, the decision to enter the franchise came into being.

This was also the time when a lot of people were just testing the waters, and there was a lot of uncertainty surrounding the franchise business. There were many speculations that the business model would explode the market absolutely. Some said this was not for a market like that of the UK and that it would collapse in a matter of years.

I knew that this business was going to work, and especially the coffee thing was not getting outdated any time soon.

Life often demands taking a leap of faith. In my particular case, that leap of faith was getting into the coffee business. But I did that after doing lots of homework. I had been studying coffee franchises lately. I was convinced that this product would sell. I involved my eldest brother in this business too, and together we started researching it. We shared our views together and embarked on making it happen. Our tour to Australia was a win-win where we learned everything about the business and signed the deal on paper.

As profit-making as it was, there were still many risks involved, the biggest one being *"We have to see how franchises perform in the UK"*. However, I was adamant about going ahead because my calculation told me this was going to be super successful. Back at home, my wife and mother were there to stand by me in this difficult decision. When I disclosed my future business plans to them, they offered their views on it and extended their complete support that helped me get on with it.

We knew there were risks involved. Hence as a backup plan, we decided to keep our store. Mina held my hand and told me she would run the store until my coffee business was

176

all set and making stable profits. It was relieving to know I was covered in the financial sense. For the time being, we decided to pay all our expenses with the earnings coming from the convenience store and save the income from the coffee business for future investments and expansion. Now, I did not have to fret over household affairs, matters pertaining to the convenience store, or running the home successfully.

What made me enter the franchise business was that there was little risk involved. This was one of the biggest push factors. If I failed, I would not lose my entire life's savings, and since I was sharing the business with my brother, I was investing half of the amount. So, all in all, it was not that big of a deal; we could take the risk. Another thing about it was that the profit margin was high. Thirdly, this business was easy to start with. We did not need to have a lot of technical know-how to get started. All we needed was a couple of machines and a handful of dedicated employers, which we managed to get with little effort.

You might be wondering why I picked coffee out of a thousand other things. I did not do that impulsively, for sure. I think mathematically, and as per my calculations, coffee was one of the best products out there. I knew beforehand that, if anything, I'd be entering the food market. The profit

177

margins are good for one reason. And the business never falls out of favour for another. The demand for food is always there in all ages at all times. People consumed food yesterday. They eat food today. They'll buy food tomorrow and always. So, here was a market that was never going out of fashion.

In those days, we used to sell a cup of coffee at a very low price. It used to be a pound of 2 and a half or three. Hence, the profit was low per cup. But we did not sell a few cups. We would sell many hundreds of them. Say, for instance, we made one pound on a cup; we would be making hundreds of pounds on hundreds of cups. Because this was a highly sought after beverage with such a low price, people would not think twice before spending money on it. Some would have it again and again. And that is how the demand kept on increasing.

Another reason why I was inclined toward coffee was that it was the perfect beverage for the evolving lifestyle of people in our part of the world. This was the time when shopping centres and malls were thronged by people every single day. Those who went shopping had money in their pockets. While shopping, they would crave light snacking and caffeine. That was when you made sure their cravings were satiated and you got business in return. They could consume their coffee while on the shopping spree.

People in the UK could not have alcohol during shopping. They could not have fizzy drinks. Those were not very appropriate for the weather. The best beverage option this class of people had was coffee. Coffee was a unanimous beverage in Australia and the USA. A lot of things that factored in making the most favourite beverage were there in the UK too. So, there was little doubt surrounding its projected success.

Not only those who were on the shopping spree had coffee, people working at offices needed to stay awake and active. They, too, would come to our place and grab a cup of coffee on their way to the office. Working around the clock and consuming caffeine was the lifestyle that was taking over the entire UK back in the day. Therefore, coffee was going to be high in demand, and we hit the market at the right time with our franchise.

With ease come challenges is as accurate in business as it is in life in general. When we were going to open our first shop, we needed a considerable amount of money. The investment and banking environment was very different in those days. This was the time when nobody was willing to take the risk for you. The 90s was a period of recession. The business environment wasn't very healthy. There was lots of chaos and uncertainty surrounding everything. Starting a business in those days was a bold decision. But keep this in mind – you have to take risks if you want to achieve something big in life. Running a convenience store would not make me a millionaire, but this coffee franchise could, so let's do it with proper research and planning, of course.

We went to the bank to get a loan. At that time, the bank lent us 30 %, and we had to put our 70 % in by ourselves. There were barely any other entities apart from banks that could invest money in our idea. Even the interest rate was very high. So, the amount we would return to the bank was going to be much higher than what we borrowed. That was yet another risk. But we took it because we were sure it was the right time to launch coffee franchises in the UK. Had we wasted some more years, the market would have got more competitive.

When you are investing so much money into something, there's no point jumping in without having a full-fledged plan. My plan was that I would find a good location for the franchise because the location brings in customers. My choice was near a shopping mall, and we managed to find one. Next, we made sure we hired dedicated and mature staff. Finally, we spend much of our time and energy training the staff perfectly so that there was no compromise on the quality of the product and service delivery. It was a beverage – the service delivery had to be super quick.

With everything in place, we got ready to design our first shop. The style was simple. There was a large counter where customers would come and place their orders. At the back of the counters would be our employees who would note down the orders and make the coffee in the machine instantly. Then they would wrap the order in nice packaging and hand it over to the takeaway customers. On the sides and at the centre would be nice and comfortable chairs and tables for the customers to sit and have their coffee on. Professionally designed menu cards would be displayed at different points so the customers could decide their order fast and easy.

My daily routine was to wake up around 6' or 6:30 and be there at the shop at around. Coffee, muffins, and sandwiches were something people needed every now and then. So, from 7:30 in the morning to the evening, we were covered. The first thing I did was buy the stock. Then, I would brief my employees. After that, when customers started coming, I'd observe them and my staff and see if there was something I could still do to improve the service delivery.

The starting time in this business was reasonable. During those days, there was a concept that if you wanted to pull off business successfully, you'd have to start at 3'o clock in the morning. Here, I could start making money at 8'o clock. The timings were quite convenient. Most days, I would be back after the evening or at night. Some days, it took longer in the shop when work related to finances or accounts had to be done. That's when I'd come home to find my daughters sleeping, and their innocent faces gave me the courage to keep going.

In the initial days, I would offer a helping hand in anything that needed an extra employee. We did not have a large number of employees; we had a sufficient number. That makes this business labour convenient too. Gradually, we made our operations more efficient, and a time came when I only had to oversee the affairs.

When we opened our first shop, I was so excited to get it rolling. Everybody else was so excited. I'd go from counter to counter to oversee the work. I'd make sure everything was in place – all the supplies were there to last us for the day at least. I wanted to ascertain the staff was motivated enough to carry out day to day tasks and meet the targets. For this purpose, I would often give them a pep talk before starting the work. During the day, I would oversee the shop for cleanliness and other mandatory things.

While walking around the shop, I would be all ears to my employees. I'd be open to all sorts of opinions, complaints, and suggestions. Since these were the people who were adept at their specific jobs, they sometimes gave really helpful information that I could use to improve my business.

Taking customers' feedback was of primary importance. We had written as well as oral means of taking their feedback. They were the ones who were paying for our product. Their views on it were most important. Likewise, solving their complaints was of prime importance because they brought us money. If we ignored them, we would only lose them, and no sane businessman would want to lose the customers.

That is how our first coffee shop took off. With time, our exposure and understanding of this business broadened, and that helped boost our business even more.

Chapter 17: One Down, Two More

Perhaps the best feeling in the world is to see your hard work bearing fruit. The pleasure is magnified when you ran against the flow to make it happen and when there were the most critical decisions involved. In my story, the success of the first shop was the only thing I looked forward to when I got into the business. There was so much at stake, and so much tension erupted within my social circle with the idea of exploring unchartered territories of franchises, and the very decision of embarking on this endeavour became the most critical thing in life.

When you aim at a grand target, rest assured that you will be faced with an unnatural amount of discouragement and attacks. Talking about that, I remember the first wave of discouragement that hit us came from none other than the people of our own community, people who were friends to us. *"Oh, these guys (My brother and I)! They're gonna buy BB's franchise, and they're gonna lose their own BBs someday,"* was what we used to hear.

If you're not an Indian, you probably didn't get the spiteful attack enclosed in these words. To explain, the franchise we were going to buy was called BB's coffee and muffin, and in Hindi, we use BB for 'wife'.

Now, put these words in the sentence above and feel the bitterness. Imagine what I would have thought and felt. This was when I did not know the art of doing business very well. At best, I had run a convenience store, and that was it. Unlike other people, I had little to no guidance at my disposal. I was all on my own. Coupled with that, I had the responsibility of my mother, wife and my daughters. My family was growing at that time and I needed to provide for them. How could somebody in my position undertake a risky ride?

As I've already mentioned in the previous chapters, the franchise business was beginning to emerge in our part of the world back then. It was a risky endeavour, but success in the same would translate into enormous prosperity. In my community, I was changing the tides by getting the entry ticket first time ever. If I succeeded, I'd wear the crown to be the first mover in my vicinity. If I didn't, I'd become the most terrible case study in the books of history.

So, it was difficult. There were lots of tensions in our society. People were busy spewing negativity. BB's coffee and muffin could give immense profits or make us lose the little possessions we had. If you haven't still figured out what the above remark means, here's the explanation. People thought my brother and I were going to end up in bankruptcy and end up losing our wives and families to abject poverty.

Such remarks made me worry. They would have made anybody think twice, thrice and more until they decided against investing in the business. However, people's discouraging views weren't the only thing bothering us. The list of cons was much longer. Another irritant in line was the constant reminder that I hadn't made enough money to survive if the franchise didn't work or failed to make ample money. If it didn't work, we wouldn't have any resources left to fall back on. If you remember, we had already taken a loan from the bank. That had to be returned too.

Investing in another business in case the first one didn't work wasn't an attractive option because then we would have lost all our savings, and accumulating every single penny for the second time would take ages. Investing the same in another risky venture would require fresh piles of motivation. All these questions and scenarios were playing in my mind until one day when I just got the response: "No matter what happens, we will take this up, and we will make this a success".

It was just a matter of time that we got everything done and were all ready to open our first shop in a busy shopping mall. As exciting as it was, it was super tense, too, in many ways, during the time when we were deliberating over the prospects of this business' success and thinking from all perspectives. There were many sleepless nights, multiple moments of doubt, and many elements of fear creeping in my brain and racing all the way down, giving the most serious jitters.

What happens when you're playing on the line is that you have to take all perspectives into account. My brother and I had invested everything in our first shop. We had to make it successful over our dead bodies. We were ready to sleep in the shopping centre every night if we had to make it churn out money for us. We were willing to do anything in our power to make it profitable. People's words made our resolve all the stronger. I'd lie in bed with their words ringing in my ears, "This is not going to work", "You'd lose everything, Shashi", "The only thing this path leads to is bankruptcy". Sigh! The more negativity they expressed at our plans, the stronger the resolve to make it successful became.

Things could never get clear until we launch it and see it taking its right course. Luckily for us, that happened quicker than we expected. When we opened our first shop, we knew we were on the right track. Our customers were enthralled by what we offered. They were beginning to develop a taste for coffee. They tried it; they liked it. In the first few weeks, it became crystal clear that coffee was here to stay and that our choice was right.

Kudos to our entire team; our products were selling like hotcakes. Every single day, people would walk inside the shop, have chit chat sessions with their friends over a cup of coffee and muffins and leave positive feedback. Coffee was becoming the new shopping partner for many. A number of them would come with shopping bags in their hands and order coffee to refresh themselves for another round of spree. We saw customers walking in regularly and leaving with a smile on their faces, and that was the assurance we needed to keep going harder.

While receiving the much-awaited positive feedback from the customers, we realised many apprehensions were just groundless. When I thought more about it, I realised people had other reasons for keeping me far from a magnificent venture. Most of the people in our friend's circle and community would run convenience stores. Their minds were smaller. They just could not envision the possibility of a franchise making money. Most of them weren't risk-takers. Hence, they would only discourage a brave move.

Also, I was new in the country. It was difficult for people to fathom that a newbie who had recently settled in the UK and barely knew enough of the culture was going to playing on a bigger canvass than they ever had.

Back at the store, everything was going well. We were selling food items that were increasingly being accepted by the people. We started with few things that we could freshly prepare and serve hot with coffee. It was a complete lunch menu. The main item was coffee. Apart from coffee, we offered muffins, sandwiches, Paninis, and a variety of drinks. It was a full-fledged lunch menu. Not too heavy, nor too light. Just perfect for a refreshing pause in between shopping.

The menu size was small. That gave us time to prepare the available products in time and manage the supplies efficiently. Fewer items, better management was one of the reasons for our efficiency. Another was the staff. We had hired middle-aged, serious and dedicated workers, and that decision proved just right when we saw them working as diligently as ourselves. They would be at the shop on time, take orders right, deal with customers politely, were always responsive and efficient in their work. Their efforts gave a strong boost to the sales.

Meanwhile, we were all growing and learning fast. It's not that we didn't do anything wrong. We did make a couple of mistakes, but our success laid in taking lessons from them

189

and rectifying the inaccuracies. There were frequent discussion sessions between our staff members and us. They would inform us of anything they saw wrong or vice versa, and together, we ascertained to fix it. Had we gone for the 'You did this wrong' or 'It's your fault' approach, making a good fix wouldn't have been possible.

Every single day brought in new learning experiences for us. We got some of the most valuable lessons in the shops. That was also the place where we acquired considerable skills. Dealing with customers with respect, treating them nicely, apologising if something was wrong on our part, making up for our mistakes by offering some extras were commonplace in our book of codes of conduct. Those were the things that made us better at public dealing and sharpened our client handling skills.

Business required unlearning and relearning of a number of things. Although prior business experience had equipped me with due management and communication skills, running a busy shop that was making higher profits was another ball game altogether. Here, I had to expand my horizon to know about the problems that came up and find quick solutions on a daily basis. Multiple unprecedented issues would pop up, and we had to resolve them efficiently.

Learning the rules of this game and adopting them was a lot of fun. It afforded us the mental nourishment we needed to become successful entrepreneurs. Thanks to the maturity of our staff and our attitude with them, we were spared incidences of intra-business conflicts. With that give, our focus was solely on polishing our service and expanding the clientele by that.

Every day was a better day than the previous one in terms of our service, modes of dealing with clients, and efficiency. With time, the feedback also kept improving. It was massively positive. Customers would come back to us way more often. They wanted a beverage that was not very expensive so they could have many cups in a day. It also went well with the British weather. You could have 10 cups a day, and you won't think you had too many.

Not just our regular customers, new people also showed up every day. People were coming from nearby towns to have our coffee and enjoy it. That gave us the positivity we needed to perform the best. Just a couple of months ago, we were worrying ourselves sick about the future of our business, and now it was taking off like a rocket.

When something works so well, what's the most natural thought that comes to the minds of the owners? Expand it. In a couple of years, I began dreaming of increasing our shops and having a bigger presence. "People are liking our coffee. I think that's our cue to expand". I discussed the option with my brother, who shared my vision and gave a heads up.

Our day to day deliberations came to a beautiful conclusion, "Why not open another shop in the town nearby? It's only ten miles away from here." My brother and I decided to go for it. We could oversee the affairs there due to close proximity and pay equal focus on its functioning. We had a little bit of experience on our belts now, and that was going to help us establish the second shop and make it running.

We would have regular discussions on how we want shop fitting to be done, where should we placed the equipment, etc. All the answers came from our experiences at the first shop. Somebody or the other would remind us that we set the counter wrong the first time; let's put it right here this time. Multiple other aspects came up, and we sorted out everything with a healthy discussion over a cup of coffee.

Chapter 18: On My Own

It was just a matter of time that the first shop converted into three shops in our name. Or maybe we were so busy getting the hang of the tools of the trade that we got numb to the passage of time. Perhaps all we could feel was that we were growing fast as new businessmen and with us, the shop was growing too.

It was almost surreal how the business progressed, keeping in view the jitters we had just before diving into the coffee business. Only a couple of years back in time, we weren't sure how successful we were going to be or if we were going to be prosperous with it. As far as I remember, we hoped it would do better numbers than a convenience store, but businesses have no guarantee. In our case, the future seemed fuzzier because we didn't see any signs of a similar set-up on the business landscape.

Before getting into the coffee franchise model, we were quite divided in our views. There was an option that each of us, my brother and I, would get a convenience store rather than a coffee shop. But after due discussions and deliberations, the central issue that came forward was the canvass we wanted to play on. A convenience store, no matter how grand you make it, would produce profits within a defined range. There's not much scope in it. A coffee shop, on the other hand, could generate mega amounts and expand like mushrooms.

That is when entrepreneurship came into play. A true entrepreneur looks at the sky. He would always choose the business whose growth capacities know no bounds. Being an entrepreneur, my eyes were set on the franchise business as I knew the scope was much larger. However, my brother did not have an entrepreneurial mindset. He was the exact opposite of mine in that respect, and that was going to result in a clash of minds in the near future.

Both my brother and I were put to the test in the coffee franchise. We were keeping close eyes to make sure every corner runs properly. We had to ensure that enough planning and effort were put into every aspect of the business to make it successful. We were managing money, orders, customers, food, and expenses for the first time. We made sure no food was wasted, the supply to available, the staff was fine, and the service was quick and efficient. The first shop was exhilarating.

It was also our very first experience of employing the staff. An entrepreneur knows who to employ and how to manage the human resource at the office. In the convenience store, it was only my wife and me who were doing everything from start to finish. But here, at the coffee shop, we employed men to do their respective jobs. That time was crucial for acquiring human resource management skills that would make us adept businessmen. All in all, there was an entrepreneur in the making.

The entrepreneur in me realised the need to be ahead of the game. In line with that thought, we made sure the planning for the next day was done beforehand. It was not tangible things alone that had to be carefully placed for the coming day; the staff needed to be ready and motivated for the next day as well. We would look into their attendance, their problems, their complaints, and their requests. If the person in charge of cleaning was going to be absent, we had to get somebody to do his job. And the time we got for arranging everything was short. So, that's where the test of our skills, patience, and attitude was.

With the success of the first shop, we were quick to open up another one. Now that my brother and I knew how to run a coffee shop, we were confident about the second one. With this expansion, the most natural thing that followed was the division of labour. My brother was going to run one shop and I the other. Now the entrepreneur was more refined and had the entire shop to be run all by himself. Here, too, I was overseeing every single operation to make sure everything was top-notch. Some more tests followed until I knew it was time for opening more shops.

The idea of having a third store was both enticing and worrying at the same time. Enticing because the entrepreneur in me always wanted to expand and blow the profits out of this business. Worrying because the two of us were already occupied with two stores, who was going to run the third one. So, this was the first time we were going to run a shop without being there. We did have cold feet at the idea, but then what do entrepreneurs do? They can't be omnipresent. They run their businesses afar and do a great job at it.

Around the same time, multiple other things were happening in life. Those were the days when the convenience store wasn't giving good numbers in profit. Perhaps it was the overall economic environment that didn't prove very productive for small businesses like that of a convenience store; investing further in them was not even an option. Hence, in my resolve to move ahead and focus all on the coffee franchise, I got rid of the convenience store. It was not making much money anyway.

The next big thing was buying my own house. With profits from the coffee shops and our savings, we moved into a new house. As my girls grew, we needed more space, and

I had been meaning to own a property in my name for a long time. So, buying a new house was the big move forward. At the same time, however, our income got limited because, after such a huge investment in the house, most of the amount was going back into the business.

In my situation, a lot of other people would have called it quits for expansion and focused on saving. But I chose to invest further. I knew we needed to build more shops, so we could grow our profits to new heights. I talked to my brother, *"We need to move on. We must expand now"*. I knew it was high time we took the bold move because the environment was perfect for expansion. It was super friendly for businesses, particularly franchises. Our franchise was already booming. We just needed to make the right decision at the right time.

My brother, who was an educated accountant, did not quite like the idea. Every time I talked about expansion, his feet got cold. The way he looked at it was the polar opposite of mine. He always looked at numbers. If the numbers were not showing hope, he wouldn't make a move. He would deliberate over the prospects of it, do his numerical research, think about it, and refuse to take the risk. Being a pessimist to the core, he always thought we would only incur losses if we moved any further than three shops.

I, on the other hand, wanted to push the button when I saw the opportunity and not wait for the right time because *"There's no right time. The only right time is now"* is what I told my brother. My belief was simple, *"I will not wait for the tide, or I'd be washed away"*. What followed was a clash between an entrepreneurial mind and the mind of an accountant.

On the topic of expansion, we had a big disagreement. One wanted to go east; the other was planning for the west. We were so much at loggerheads with each other that there was no middle ground between our differing, rather opposing, views. This was not the first time that we differed in our approaches. Earlier, there was a time when we were offered a site in a mall close to our home. There was no way a shop at such a populous location would fail. Following my instinct, I tried hard to convince my brother to buy it and open a shop there.

However, my brother was quite slow, pessimistic, and he only trusted the picture numbers gave him. I never liked being slow and keep leaving out opportunities. But, there was no way I could go ahead alone while in partnership with him. So, naturally, we lost the site to someone else who took the timely decision of buying it.

Soon after, the guy who bought it started doing big numbers, and I was only left with regrets. I had a word with my brother and explained that if we kept losing opportunities like that, we'd end up nowhere. I also tried to explain that nothing in life was guaranteed. If we ran after security, we would only fool ourselves and lose everything. Business is all about taking risks. We should have known that from the time we signed up for it.

Now when expansion was the issue where the shoe pinched. By this time, I had made up my mind to go ahead in the face of adversity. I'd not lose any more opportunities, even if that meant going alone. The next few days made it clear that we were going to go our own ways. Being good brothers, we shook hands and decided that nothing would affect our relations with each other on a personal level, and we would part ways peacefully.

It was the year 2000 when we split. Going on my own way gave me a license to print money. I had good relations with the bank manager and everybody associated with the business. I was known as the fast and furious man who would grab opportunities as they came his way and make them work for him. Now, I was free to do anything out of my free will. I felt relieved and empowered.

Sometimes in business, you have to stand by tough decisions to reap sweeter fruits in the future. Being an entrepreneur, I understood that it was the need of the hour. I felt very positive about the split. Back at home, my wife and young daughters had my back. During our long discussions on the topic, they always expressed unity with my thoughts and plans.

Thanks to my mother's and my wife's upbringing, my daughters had the maturity to respect their uncle like they would when we were partners. Similarly, my love and respect for my brother did not change even for a minute. We were civilised enough not to let the business clash affect our personal relationship.

My mother had passed a year before the split. Luckily, she did not see us parting ways with her own eyes. Otherwise, it would have been very painful for her. She had always wanted us to grow together at the same pace. She wanted us to collaborate in every matter, perhaps more so in business. I remember telling Mina, *"Look, Mina, mom's not here anymore. What is going to happen is going to happen. Let's make the tough decision and go our own way in the business. I'm sure we can do a lot better than what we're doing now".*

When I make a decision, I put my hundred per cent into it and make it succeed. That is the quality that keeps me going and acing every endeavour I get myself into. I knew that going alone would be hard, but I barely had any option but to work hard till my shop was blowing the profits I visualised. I believe when you put all your energy into making something work, instead of fretting over its prospects or worrying about failure, there's no reason you would fail. At the end of the day, the choice is yours.

I was left with a single shop after the split. The year 2000 was heaven for businesses. I immediately borrowed money from the bank and made it two shops in my name. One I got, another one I made. With that, I was running two shops all on my own for the very first time. I asked myself, *"Am I relying on my educated brother, or have I got the ability to carry on and build the business?"*

The answer came naturally. I didn't have the education, but I was willing to put in an immense amount of hard work. I was never afraid of working hard, and neither was my wife. We weren't going to take no for an answer. We were going to make it.

With that in mind, I built a strong team. Together, we took the operation, administration, and expansion upon ourselves. We took everything under one umbrella and made sure we had all answers. We knew what was happening in the business. It took me a couple of years to learn the hardest lessons of business. After all, my brother and I had been in partnership for five long years. This time around, I really wanted to know for myself that I could know all aspects of running a business in and out.

The first two years of working solo were good training. I went there every day, worked with all the employees, and got to know every aspect and every person. It was the same thing I was doing there, only that I was in complete control now, and my responsibility increased manifold. In those years, I learned things that my brother used to oversee previously and developed strong networks with my staff and with other relevant people.

Before I could expand, I needed to know the business through and through. Then a time came when my bank accounts were healthy, and I had put skilled staff to work on the technical side of the business, such as the bank accounts, returns, etc.

My business was the one-man army. As challenging as it sounds, it was equally exciting. It was almost like a dream coming to fruition. Now, I was all by myself. Whatever decisions I took were going to be final. If I wanted to buy more sites and open more shops, there was nobody who could tell me to do otherwise. Above all, I had the support of my wonderful wife and my young daughters. All of us were willing to put in whatever hard work it required or make any sacrifices that the time demanded.

I call myself an entrepreneur, but time proved that my wife and daughters were no less than that in their thinking. That and the newfound liberty in business gave me a powerful push to keep going forward.

Chapter 19: Expansion

I still close my eyes sometimes, and the flashbacks of my brother and I having conversations regarding entering a bigger business play before my eyes. *"We should look for a business which would help us multiply our streams of income". "With the money we get, we could improve our standard of living". "Yes, as my girls are growing up fast, it is just a matter of time that I'd need money to finance their education". "Absolutely! And with a business up and running, we can finance our vacations and holidays too".*

So, this was the plan. The universe had other plans and from a single business paying enough to finance our expenses, I went to open not less than thirty-five shops. Now, when I think of it, I cannot help admiring how long how I came this far. Perhaps when we actually entered the real business, the entrepreneur in me took over, and the rest is history.

Just like a vampire tastes blood and craves it all the more ferociously, I had tasted the miracles of money and I wanted more of it now. My brother and I, when we got into it, began to witness the miracles of its expansion. Hence, we realised there was enormous potential in this business. That led us to go to the bank and take more money to open more shops. I was thinking of building an empire and my brother was focused on creating some extra sources of income to finance our expenditures. That was the unbridgeable difference between us.

When we were at three, my brother's thirst got satiated. But the entrepreneur in me had known the art of making money and would not stop at any cost. What fueled the desire further were the characteristics I had, such as risk taking, thinking ahead of the game, making smart calculations, and willingness to keep going. As I've already explained, they clashed with those of my brother, and we parted our ways in business happily.

Now, the fire in me got stronger. Being on my own taught me the skills I needed to run the business without any external help. I soon became the jack of all trades. Now, I did not look left or right; I just focus on expanding the business. I went slowly till five shops because those years were spent learning all aspects of the work and testing the waters. Once I knew I was good to go, I wanted to go harder and more aggressively in the business, and this was the right time to do exactly that.

As they say, a true entrepreneur has to be daring. They should be confident about their idea and have the courage to go ahead with them. As an entrepreneur, my first most daring step was to double my shops from five to ten. Within a year, my income doubled because my shops doubled. Now, I started understanding how a business ran without the owner sitting in the shops all day long.

With the expansion, the responsibility multiplied. Back at work, I was doing multiple jobs at the same time. Every single day was like running a marathon. I was motivating my workers to do their work as good as they could. I had not one or two but ten shops to look after. I made sure I went shop by shop and oversee their work and motivate my employees. We were doing more work and achieving more milestones on a daily basis.

Building connections with my staff was a crucial part of the business. We were a family of highly bonded people. There were about 2000 people at one time that were working for me, and I was in contact with every one of them. I knew all of my staff by name. They were like a family to me. I told my employees, *"If there's any problem, come to me. I'll try my best to solve it. If I can't, I'd guide you in the right direction"*. My employees knew I was there for any kind of help they needed, and hence they were there to own the place they were working at and put their best into it. That boosted our trust levels and helped us build a stronger and more reliable working relationship.

With ten stores, I could not do the kind of work I was doing with five stores. So, now, I was not working hard; I was working smart. I was getting the employees to do the work the way I wanted it to be. Naturally, that meant making multiple new appointments. I had to put operations people, area managers in the shops. I was now overseeing major positions, taking the report directly from them, and keeping a careful eye on the major areas.

That did not mean my burden lightened. Where I was doing one man's job initially, I was doing five people's jobs now. I just changed my hats as and when needed. If there was a need for a supply position, I put on the supply hat. If there was a need for operations or finance person, I quickly put on the relevant hat and started working. That was the time I had long been preparing myself. I knew while running the first two stores that I'd have to learn everything if I have to expand this empire. So, there I was, doing multiple jobs according to the needs of the shops.

I was also meeting and greeting people every day. I would pay special attention to staying in the good books of every supplier, every member, every company involved in the business. That required loads of greetings, meetings, and looking after them. I knew I had to build and maintain good relations with everybody. Anybody could come in handy when I needed help. It was like developing a mutually beneficial bond. You stand by them; they'll stand by you when you need them.

Here's a brief summary of my expansion from five to fifteen. When I separated from my brother, I had a single shop. I took baby steps from one to five shops. However, when they were five, I took a jump and got to ten. That was a 100 per cent expansion. Those five new shops required I took a million pounds loan, and I did it. At that time, there was a guarantee of about 25 per cent of the loan. So, that made my liability to be around 250,000 pounds. Within the next five months, I opened five more stores. For that, I took a loan of a quarter-million pounds. With the liability I had now, maintaining the cash flow became one of my most important priorities now.

The next big step was further increasing the number of stores from 15 to 35. This was a massive expansion. With such expansion, I had to install various check posts on the way to make sure every operation, every function was taking place nicely. Needless to say, that required lots of thinking on my part. So, the erstwhile physical effort became mental in nature. Something or the other was going on in my mind all the time. My brain couldn't switch off. I was constantly thinking on my behalf and my employees' behalf.

To succeed in business, I believe you have to be two steps ahead of the business. If you're chasing the business, then you're going to fall eventually because all you'll be doing is chasing. That is something that never ends, and hence you're never going to win the business because you'll always be behind it.

The best strategy is to let the business chase you. When you do that, your thoughts and actions have to be ahead of the business. Think about this. If you're two steps ahead of the business, you will have the solution to the problem that is going to arise tomorrow. When it comes, you'll overcome it in no time. There's no reason why you would fail when you have developed the habit of staying two steps ahead of the business. That is the key to running a business successfully.

My belief is when running a business, anything goes wrong, the repair time is very important. The shorter it is, the better. Only someone who is ahead of the business will be able to fix the inconsistencies as they arise without their customers even realising what just came. I, for one, remained prepared for fixing things in time so that the business functioned smoothly and kept churning out money.

In business, when your account is strong, the entire world is with you. Take my case, for example. I had my accounts in good shape even with two shops, and the bank was with me. That is probably why I had no problem taking loans and expanding my presence across the UK. Every time I got a loan, the monthly checking of my accounts became more strenuous. That gave me the impetus to keep going hard and fast.

Expanding a business is no easy feat. You have to keep so many entities together. You have to keep in touch with everybody who has a role in the business. When you take loans, you have to pay special attention to satisfy the banks. I, too, had to keep the bank happy. For that reason, the cash flow in my accounts had to be strong to pass the various checks the bank put. There were always hundreds of thousands of pounds in my account, and that was by no stroke of luck. I had to make sure that much money was there so that I could please the bank and expand at my will.

Did I tell you this was the time when the coffee business was going through the roof? It was the golden time for a commodity like coffee. Being a smart entrepreneur, I could not let go of the opportunity to reap the benefits of running a high-in-demand business in a business-friendly environment. There is no better favour you can do to your business than hitting the right opportunity at the right time.

I did not wait till the opportunity of expansion was gone. I made the perfect decision just in time and received multiple benefits. With 35 shops up and running, we were like printing money. Everything was on point. Every entity was doing their jobs the way I wanted them. I had to be involved more actively with each and every stakeholder that was playing some part in the business. Even in the presence of managers, I had to make sure each and every bit of my thirty-five shops was doing okay.

One of the best parts of doing this business was that I developed a very good network with others. Even though I was running a franchise, I never felt for a moment that it was somebody else's business. I always felt as if it was my own brand. It was making me good money; I had invested so much into it. I had to make it successful. Therefore, I put my best into all the affairs associated with this business.

Perhaps the juiciest part of being an entrepreneur is that you never stop learning. Be it business, self-development, health, or personal grooming, you are always acquiring new knowledge and practising it in your daily life. I remember I was always involved in other things in life apart from business. Every day was a new day, and I felt I had done justice to my life and my time when I closed my day, recalling at least some new lessons I derived from my day.

Those nine years when I was super active in the business were loaded with new experiences, learning, hard work, networking, and lots of profit. It was never a smooth process. There were innumerable ups and downs. Some days were replete with challenges; some were lighter; some were even fun. There were times when I felt really helpless, but the next day I woke up with hope in my eyes.

In the coffee business that I was in, I encountered two biggest challenges in the entire 9-year period. One of the major lessons I learnt is that business is not a problem; employees are. When you need them, they won't show up. When there are busy weekends coming, they won't take your calls and remain absent from duty.

Saturdays are busy in a mall. What happened was the employees got paid on Friday. So, Friday night was mostly celebration nights. A lot of them would have alcohol and blackout. Consequently, they would not come the next day. It was a recurring thing, particularly with the younger lot. Many times, the parents of these people would call and say they would not come because they were not feeling well.

There was nothing more frustrating than that. When employees let you down, you barely have anybody else to fall back on. At most, you could appreciate the few workers that showed up to boost their morale. By the end of the day, those, too, would be super tired, and that affected their efficiency.

When I started, we had more mature and serious people on board. With time, however, we made rigorous hires and kept all kinds of people when different ideas emerged from the US and other parts of the UK regarding hiring more younger people. In the beginning, loyalty and reliability were the highest among the employees. They would not mind coming early and putting extra hours to work because they were extremely committed to their jobs. However, with time, these traits got really thin.

Another thing that bothered me a lot was related to the supply. As I explained, weekends were busy in malls, so there was more business on these days, and we needed supplies to meet the demand of the customers. However, around that time, a lot of the stores had run out of supplies. We asked them to provide us with a list of items, and we hardly got everything.

Those two things I found the hardest to deal with because there was not much I could do about it. I had to keep trying to get the items we needed for the weekend and encourage the on-job employees to work hard. That was all I could do. Apart from these, everything else was manageable. All the other problems came and went; these two were the most recurring ones.

The time from 2000 to 2014 was a brilliant time for my business. We grew by leaps and bounds. By this time, I was running it alone. Now the time had come when that needed to change. My business was going to become our family business now.

Before we talk about the family business further, let's have a look at some pictures from the time we were expanding the business.

Chapter 20: A Family Business

With 15 stores in full swing, I was super happy and excited at the same time. My dream of making lots of money had become a living reality, and I, along with my family, was living the life I had always aspired for. My bank accounts were healthy; we could afford costly education for my daughters and have vacations in the best places around the world. Everything was going just right. The only difficulty I was facing pertained to running the businesses, and even that was something I had gotten quite accustomed to by this time.

Perhaps I would be operating a chain of franchises under the tag of BB Coffee and Muffins to this day if fate had not put challenges on my way and I had not taken the right decisions in those times. As they say, an entrepreneur looks for opportunities and avails them before everybody else out there does. Life presented me with different circumstances, and just in line with this thought, I again made some critical decisions for the future of my business. Before we delve into those decisions, let's understand the business climate of that time.

This was the year 2008. Does that ring a bell? Yes, it was the time of the Great Recession. During this time, the world was witnessing a global economic downturn. As a result, financial markets, banking and real estate sectors came into severe crises in the UK and elsewhere. The poor performance of most markets affected the business owners and employers. What came next was thousands of people losing their jobs, their savings and their homes.

As we know, businesses do not operate in isolation and cannot stay unaffected by the broader geo-economic and political changes shaping the landscape of the entire globe's economy. The Great Recession was a global phenomenon, and none of the businesses could stay immune from its adverse implications. Think about this. When people don't have money, they won't be interested in buying anything that's more than a necessity. So, we could see our business treading on dangerous ground in the near future.

The most relevant question for us was: What could recession mean for a franchise business? At the back of my mind, there was this thought doing the rounds that *"This is not my brand. This is somebody else's, and I am just running it"*. If people reduced coffee consumption, which looked inevitable now, our business would suffer. From the money that I got, I could not keep the entire amount; hence, my profit would reduce naturally. Also, I could not expand this franchise at my own will, and nobody knew how long the recession was going to last. Maybe one year, maybe two, maybe five. All in all, it was going to be a dicey situation for franchisees.

Such hits are part of life, but an entrepreneur should know what their next move should be and how quickly they want to make it. Just when the recession began, I started weighing my options. I realised that I had already taken this business to its peak and now was the best time to sell it. That was indeed a tough decision, and working toward achieving it was even tougher.

In a bid to get buyers, we started approaching corporate giants. We presented our business model before them and tried convincing them on making a purchase. Some sounded interested; others were clearly not. We presented our case to quite a number of them and expected positive development on that.

Around 2009, our franchisor went into administration. What that meant was my franchises, and all the others of the same name had an administrator above them who would direct our functions in many respects.

It was the time when a lot of people started taking prominent sites, so I had to get up the ground very quickly. I was hiring architects, agents to speak on my behalf in a frenzy. I was meeting the prospects and getting to meet different people who I knew from some connection or who were a part of my social network to take care of different aspects of my work that I could assign them.

About that time, lots of positive things had happened inside the home. My eldest daughter, Dimple Patel, had gotten married, and I got an amazing son-in-law, Vikesh Patel. Both of them were highly qualified and were working at different corporations in the private sector. My son-in-law was working at JP Morgan and had been my son-in-law for a couple of years and my daughter was working for Goldman Sachs as a trader.

Just when we were trying to sell a good number of our shops, another idea clicked on us. By that time, my franchises occupied important locations in the city. They were doing good numbers, and we could do better if we put a new name to them and made them our own. So, we had our shops at prime locations, and we had increased manpower to manage the business. Maybe we could make a bigger move. That's when the thought of building our own brand started hitting me ferociously. If we took this course, we could expand to the rest of the country and multiply our numbers.

I would call it a mega opportunity. In times of distress, there are two options. One, you can quit the struggle. Two, you can work out a plan to use the challenges to your advantage and get started. Although I did try to avail the first option, some part of me wanted to explore the second, despite coming this far.

There was a shift in the story now. I was not the only entrepreneur in my family anymore. I had two young people join me in taking this idea forward. The moment I discussed it with Dimple and Vikesh, they were exhilarated. They were not in favour of getting a lump sum and sleeping on it. They wanted to play the game, and so did I. Together, the three of us fasten our seatbelts, determined to go nationwide.

Sooner than we realised, we were a team of three people. In this team, I was the experienced one, and the two of them were highly qualified and extremely hard-working individuals. They were entrepreneurs in the making. The two did not have much exposure to leading a business, but they were willing to put in the extra amount of hard work in the business. They were so dedicatedly involved in work that they quit their jobs and resolved to give our business their one hundred per cent.

The economic environment made us took desperate steps. It was almost as if we decided to go out there and open our own brand overnight. A couple of days back, there was no such plan. But as they say, nature has its own schemes. If the recession had not come, I would not have thought of launching my own brand and the franchise business would never have been converted into our family business.

Making a decision is one thing; working for it to make it successful is another. Now, we entered step two of creating our own brand. We needed to get it registered, meet the suppliers, work on the stores, come up with an exciting design, and get the marketing work done. Again, I found myself travelling around the city, meeting suppliers, giving orders, making extensive plans, redoing every single detail to add uniqueness to our brand.

As any good team would do, we divided duties among ourselves. My daughter and son-in-law were good with finances and marketing, they took care of those areas, and I was adept at dealing with suppliers, so I focused on that. It was not an easy task. We were working extra hard. We used to work more than sixty hours per week work. There were no offs; there were no breaks; there was no escaping the work. However, we were bent on making it a success.

Now came the strategy formation part. Our method was to identify the targets, make a plan to achieve the same, and appoint the person who could do it best. So, here we go. We knew we desperately needed to expand to the south, so we had a clear target. This work was something my son-in-law could do nicely, so we gave him this responsibility. He was going to focus on the south, and we were to oversee the matters here.

While running franchises, you don't usually have centralised operations. But having your own business requires you to have a central office from where you operate. So, while we were executing expansion plans, we also moved into our own office. Before that, I was operating from home. Now, we had a full-fledged office in London, and we appointed the staff required to work at it.

We kept going little by little, and we were getting stronger each passing year. We opened locations at different places, hired the staff, talked to the suppliers, set working standards, and managed the different shops we had at different locations. The economic situation also improved gradually. 2011 was a good year. 2012 and 2013 were even better. And then came 2012.

If you are a sports fan, you probably know that the 2012 Olympics were hosted by the UK. Thousands of people thronged to London to attend the four weeks long Olympics. Luckily, we had a site at the international train station, and thanks to the Olympics, people were visiting us like bees to swarms. We made crazy sales during that time of the year. We were closing at 3 and opening at 6 o'clock in the morning those days.

Preparing for a mega-event needed mega planning. Naturally, hiring lots of staff, managing a greater number of supplies, and planning for busier days was all that was on our minds. This was such a buzzing time that the customers kept coming and going. We barely had time to take a pause. There was a line of those waiting to get their coffees. We fell short of space for accommodating the number of people that were coming, and they were constantly rising.

In a matter of years, we were everywhere. We had created a brand that was doing great. So, we were going from strength to strength. We did not have anything to limit our expansion. Unlike the franchise business, this was our own brand, Love Coffee, and we could not be more proud to have it spread across the length and width of the UK.

You might be wondering that our family business rocked since day one because Shashi Patel was a pro at managing coffee shops. Well, that is not the reality. Everything takes time to function smoothly and to bear profits. The same happened with us. In fact, in the first twelve to eighteen months, my daughter and my son in law were just learning the ins and outs of the business.

Earlier, they had worked in big corporations. However, their role was quite limited and specialised there. Here, on the other hand, they had to learn each and every aspect of the coffee business to be able to run it profitably. Being new to this world, they took time to get the hang of it, but they did learn all its aspects because they were committed to it. Coupled with that, they were also dedicated and persistent.

One of the biggest achievements of my life was developing the 'Love Coffee' enterprise. It was the result of the efforts of my entire family and me. Our collective efforts enabled us to have a brand of our own and make it known to the people out there.

A large part of your success is marketing. Where your efforts are important, marketing is perhaps equally contributing to success, if not more so. There are multiple coffee brands out there, but coffee lovers might don't know them all. They know you; they'll buy from you. Somebody else might have a better product, but their chances of being hunt down are meagre if their marketing is weak. Knowing that, we got our marketing strong and made our name known to the customers so that they buy from us.

The environment of the 1990s was very different from today. Back then, we didn't have social media or the internet like we have today. So, one of the key things we focused on was to exploit the various marketing platforms we had so that our product was known to a large majority. In doing that, the newer generation, which included my daughter and son-in-law, came in handy. They understood what the need of the hour was and worked hard towards meeting it.

The three of us made the perfect team. My expertise in the business and those of my children in modern methods prove very fruitful, and to this day, we have numerous shops serving our brand. As for profits, we made big numbers. There was a time when we were making 10 million pounds per annum of sales. Then a time came when this business became fun for us. We enjoyed the changing dynamics, altered our strategy and played the game with more excitement.

For somebody who came from India with basic education and a minimal skillset, this 10 million pounds was a mammoth achievement. If you remember the time I came here, I barely had money in my pocket and was completely dependent on my brother. I could not even speak the English language. Then, slowly and gradually, I learned the language, developed the required skills for carrying out business and took important decisions.

Looking back, I feel life was an interesting journey. Starting from zero, we built a multimillion-pounds empire. A big thanks to the ups and downs that made me take bold decisions and never look back.

Chapter 21: Challenges

Setting up a brand and spreading it to the length and breadth of London wasn't a straightforward task. Every now and then, a new problem emerged, staring us into the eyes, and we had to make a tough decision. The very decision and the entire process of launching our own brand into the market were replete with obstacles.

I remember how I used to deliberate upon this issue for long hours, thinking about all the possible pros, cons, rights, and wrongs. On the one hand, the franchise model was going down the drain in a matter of few years as it seemed, and on the other side, starting something of my own required so much extra work on my part that I wasn't entirely sure if I could fulfil all those requirements.

Just when I was going through the thought process, a painful image struck my mind. There was me holding my mother's hand, helping her through the airport stairs. I was in my late teens and was absolutely clueless as to what was going to become of me. I barely had any nice clothes to wear, but that was not a trouble. That I did not know how I was going to survive and support my mother in this place was the most tumultuous feeling.

That was the time when I hardly knew some basic words of English. If you remember, I told you in one of the earlier chapters how I learned a few expressions with a friend's help for our flight to the UK. Now, I stood there confused about what to do next. After that time, multiple moments came when I had to make a tough choice. Should I receive the education or start a business? Should I continue with a convenience store or play a bigger game? Should I continue with one shop or open more? Should I continue with my brother or part ways with him? Would it be wise to take a big loan and expand, or should I be complacent with five shops?

All in all, life had been pretty challenging all along. Now, the questions I asked myself were, "How could I give up now when I have never given up in life?" "Is this challenge bigger than my capacity?" The answer came almost naturally. "This was not a difficult thing for me; it was very much doable". "Let's do a SWOT analysis of having my own brand".

I have taken many difficult decisions in my business journey. However, the motivating factors for them have changed from time to time. When I was considering entering the franchise business, my main aim was to get everything better for my wife, mom, and my girls. The same goal guided me a long way. Later, a time came when I was in a financial position to afford pretty much a good lifestyle for my family, and now my instincts told me to take a long jump.

Of course, bigger business means more money. I would not deny that money was the primary motivating factor behind me starting my own brand, but other things added up too. For instance, I could not accept defeat. I wanted to play the game further. Also, I had such valuable lessons up my sleeves that I did not wish all that knowledge to go wasted. Finally, the entrepreneur in me spotted an opportunity in the market and was not willing to miss it.

The women of the families, like always, supported me in this tough decision. This was around 2008 when my mother had long passed away, but her legacy remained with us. Her values, principles, and teachings made us what we were, and we knew whatever decision we took, she would have stood by our side.

People have different ways of dealing with challenges. Mine is a simple one. Whenever there is a challenge facing my business, I do a careful analysis of the risks and rewards involved. When I do that, I consider all the possible dimensions of it. If the rewards are greater and more promising than the risks, I am ready to undertake whatsoever come my way. That's how we went from convenience store to coffee business.

229

I am driven by a force that tells me to avail each opportunity that comes my way. When I see one, I get so restless that I cannot stop myself from taking a dive into it. Some people want an absolute guarantee that everything would go safe and sound. They are afraid of challenges. They play safe. My brother was that kind of a person. Then there's the other type. These people take the risk and play big. They're not afraid of challenges. They enjoy the process and keep their eyes on the sky. I belong to this category of people.

Again, when it was time for me to start my own business, multiple challenges came up. One of the most initial problems pertained to my capacity. Earlier, I was running the BB Coffee and Muffins, and there, I was solely responsible for operating the business. That did not involve dealing with corporate lords. In case I managed to expand my brand to the south and elsewhere, which was the plan, I did not know how I was going to work so many shops in different places.

At BB Coffee and Muffins, I was keeping an eye on finance, accounts, employees and was dealing with every aspect of the business. However, now that my shops were not going to be in close proximity with one another, managing them was going to be a humungous task. Moreover, I was going to be responsible for operations, doing our own marketing, dealing with landlords, paying them rent, and dealing with legal affairs all on my own.

The biggest risk was that I had to be the sole responsible entity taking care of all aspects of the business. Now, many new elements added up into the equation. Doing everything myself meant I had to do rigorous planning beforehand. I planned the locations, business model, hiring, building our own office, and Mina was there to aid me with everything.

The most serious challenge that came before us was putting your own brand out in the market. That would mean entering into open competition with the corporate giants. A franchise meant you were running somebody else's brand. Launching our own brand in the market meant playing with big boys. Needless to say, we needed an excellent game plan, not just to survive but to thrive. In order to thrive, we had to have everything right. One small mistake could be very costly. So, it was like treading the path fast and carefully at the same time.

You can imagine how engaging this whole process was. There would not be a single moment when my head was not thinking about it. Day and night, I was making plans and thinking about executing them. At the back of my mind was only one thing that I had to make my business a success. No matter how many obstacles came in the way, I was not going to quit. I would work for it till it becomes a success.

I had clear targets before me. I wanted to expand to wherever we could spread the tentacles of our business. There were myriad places where the coffee business could be trendy. All of those areas I had been looking forward to exploring for quite some time. Now that I was free from all sorts of restrictions, I could expand like wildfire.

Expansion came at a later stage. Before expansion, we had to focus on building our own brand and creating our own business from scratch. Those were things I had not done before. For BB Coffee and Muffins, the brand was already there, and there was the whole model that we only had to replicate. We had to do everything, from designing the logo to coffee mugs and ensuring their ample supply for our brand. We needed to redesign our shops, their entire interior, and all the objects therein in line with the theme of our brand.

I had some consolation in the form of my existing sites. I already had some active sites at the shopping malls, which were doing great. Hence, operating them was not a big problem. The challenge came when we opened more shops bearing the new name "Love Coffee". We came up with this name because it targeted those who loved coffee. People enjoyed it from their first sip, and we wanted them to have the best experience with our coffee.

Soon after, we began marketing for our brand. We wanted people to know we existed, and we offer exactly what they wanted. We revised our menu, hired more people, organised the shops, and dealt with all stakeholders. Around the same time, working from the office had started. I would go to the office to oversee their work and address the issues when there were any.

All of the work was getting quite exhausting. After working around the clock, we felt we had no time left to focus on expansion. That was where we realised we needed more people than Mina and Me. We talked to our eldest daughter, Dimple, and son-in-law, Vikesh. The two young people were more than willing to join us. They realised carrying out our own business was the best thing. That was where they could invest their time and energy in the best way.

Just when they joined us, multiple challenges came before them too. Firstly, the targets were very high. Their background was very different. My son-in-law was working at JP Morgans, and my daughter was working for Goldman Sachs as a trader. At their jobs, they used to perform very specialised jobs. Their role was limited to specific tasks which also suited their qualifications. However, at the coffee business, they would be dealing with employees and customers, taking feedback directly from the people, framing the marketing strategy, etc. All those were tasks they were doing for the first time, yet they seemed so determined to learn everything that I could see they would be running a significant part of the business in a couple of years.

Another challenge facing Dimple and Vikesh was that they had to learn the tricks of the trade very quickly. One reason for that was we needed to expand fast. Another thing was they had to be in charge of entire shops, so the sooner they know the ins and outs of this business, the better. To aid them with work, somebody had to be there to help them with everything. Naturally, I was that somebody. I made sure I spent proper time with them explaining how the business worked, how they should deal with the people involved in it, what areas they should keep an eye on, and how they should oversee the expansion.

My daughter had seen me running this business for years, but she never quite got too involved in it. She had other things on her plate. She had school, then other activities, and later went to higher studies. After getting a degree, she pursued her career in her field. A little while after she started

234

working, she got married. So, she never got the chance to get into the coffee business, even though she had always adored it.

The same was the case with my son-in-law. He had a stellar educational background, and that's where he focused his energy for the most part. After graduation, he went off to work at a multinational firm. He did not get the opportunity or see the need to enter business either. So, now that both of them were here, they had no experience under their belt, and I was training them in the industry. They always looked up to me when they faced any trouble, and I was there to help them out.

If I talk about the risks I took, going from 15 stores to 25 stores was a risky decision. Perhaps the riskiest in the entire journey. However, again, there was an opportunity, and I could not let go of it. I did a SWOT analysis and came up with the answer, "Yes, this is going to be a mega-hit if we do these things right". Then, I did not look back any time later. I knew my targets; I knew the ways to go about them; I had the plan ready; I had the staff; all I needed to do was to keep going and make it a success.

In life and more so in business, challenges come and go, but you need to know your approach to dealing with them. You should write your priorities in black and white and be very clear about them. In my case, I was sure that I would put the business at the forefront. If something was good for the business, I would go ahead with it even if it was too much hassle for me.

In other words, I just needed to do what was most suitable for the business. The rest did not matter. For example, if I found a busy site that looked promising for the company, but which was at a place where the rent was high or finding employees was difficult, I would open a shop there. Then, I would exploit all my energy and sources to hire employees and bear with the rent. With time, the problems would dissipate, and the shop would be hugely profitable.

That is exactly what I taught my children to look at the long-term results and not to be bothered by short-term, temporary ailments. The problems will come, but an entrepreneur has their priorities right, and they aim at long-term results. When you do that, you will find ways to sort out the issues that pop up in the beginning.

Every business endeavour experiences setbacks. Even if you are not a business owner, you must have faced challenges in other areas of your life. The deal is, you have to develop the attitude of taking the bull by the horns instead of ignoring it. That would give you the courage to tackle every difficulty you encounter in your way.

Chapter 22: Heart Attack

"So, what I am planning to do is expand till we have fifty shops around the country. Once we get to that, I will sell my business and live off the fat of the land". This is something I used to tell Mina often at lunch, after coming from the office or before dosing off in the bed. She would listen quite intently to my plan and seemed happy with it. Perhaps she had already started fantasising about a life with me in which we travelled, looked after our grandchildren, spent time with family and did all the fun we missed in our youth.

In all honesty, I, too, was looking forward to the time when I would retire and Mina and I would live our lives in the most meaningful way. While chasing the 50 shops goal, I did not realise that I was running and running and losing some important things as I ran. I was laser-focused on the target that everything else blurred out of my vision. The most ignored part was my body, which was calling out for help, but I didn't pay it any heed.

Now when I reflect on my struggles in those years, I feel just like a character in one of those games that runs non stop unless they die or get caught. I was doing the same, only that I stopped before the game ended, fortunately.

It was the year 2011 when I began having pain in my left arm while working one day. I went to the doctor to find out what was wrong. They did a thorough check-up of my arm and said that it was some muscular pain. With a prescription of some medicines and physiotherapy in my hand, I left the clinic. The physiotherapist made me do a couple of exercises and arm movements. Some days passed by, but there were no signs of the pain going away. I thought maybe one day my arm would be okay.

Being a businessman meant non-stop work. I didn't have weekends off. In fact, those were the times when there was often double work. One Sunday evening, I was at home, and my body was not feeling right. I had a light chit chat with Mina and our youngest daughter, who had come to the home for the university holidays. Then, I went to bed early and instantly got asleep.

About midnight, Mina, who was sleeping next to me, observed some abnormality in my snoring. We're a funny couple. We sleep a certain way, and when there's a change in the normal sleep manner of either of us, the other spots it instantly. So, this one night, Mina was sound asleep and just in the middle of it, she heard me snoring funnily. She got up in an instant. She tried to wake me up, but I won't flinch. She got up and turned the lights on.

239

She saw me lying lifeless with my tongue sticking out. It turned out that I was in the middle of a heart attack. Seeing me in this condition made her scream in horror. My youngest daughter came running into the room. She called the hospital, and they sent an ambulance in an instant. Meanwhile, they directed her to perform CPR on me.

This was our most sensitive daughter. We used to call her softie because she was extremely soft and touchy. We could not think in the worst of our imaginations that life would put us in a situation where she would have to perform CPR on her dad. However, at the same time, I'm extremely proud that my daughter was courageous enough to do anything to help her dad survive. She did until two minutes later when the ambulance arrived.

The medical staff checked me up, and they didn't seem very hopeful. I wasn't breathing. They said the most painful thing to Mina, *"He's not breathing. Perhaps it's time you should call your family"*. My wife was devastated at that. She told the doctors that the entire family was dependent on me and requested them to give their best shot. They gave me the CPR for quite a long time until my breathing started. In the next few minutes, it stopped again, so they did another CPR there.

I was taken to the hospital in a rush. I was admitted to the special heart institution. There, they did multiple tests and discovered a blockage in the artery of my heart. I was taken to the operation theatre, where the doctors removed the blockage that had been built in the artery to clear the flow. It took them two to three hours to do so, and then they put the stunt.

I was kept unconscious for about a whole week. During this time, the doctors called my family and explained to them that one of the many things that could happen when I would wake up. My brain could be paralysed. I could have memory loss or some other terrible effect of a heart attack. My family was petrified. During this time, some of my employees who were extremely loyal to me heard the news and were so affected by the news that they kept inquiring about my health. My wife and daughters were receiving calls from people every day. These were the people I had helped in the business, or my employees or those I had good relations with.

The week passed, and it was time to wake me up. The first thing I did after waking up was I asked, *"What am I doing here?"* *"You got a heart attack"*. *"I did? No, I was sleeping. How did I come here?"* I just felt as though I had been sleeping the whole time. When I was up, I couldn't quite connect the dots. It took me a month to make sense of things.

I understand that there's no right time to die. However, there's a time when you can die without causing your entire family to crumble. When I was 47 and had a heart attack, my family depended on me, my youngest daughter was still studying, and there was nobody who would carry the business forward without any help. So, that was not the right time to be sure. Perhaps nobody would agree to die, but if given a choice, I would prefer to die when I have nobody to depend on me.

At the hospital, my daughters came to meet me, and I recognised them. The doctors were glad that I didn't have any side effects. However, I don't remember a single event from that entire week. I only remember that I was sleeping on the sofa and then went upstairs to sleep on the bed. After that, I woke up at least a week later in the hospital. In between, I don't remember anything. That particular week is blank in my diary to this day.

If you remember, I told you earlier on that I had a habit of working out. I was not one of those people who would dump wrong food in their bodies and ensconce on the chair all day long. I would exercise every day before starting work. Every day, I would walk three miles and run three. In fact, the doctors told Mina that one of the reasons my memory didn't go away was that I had a nice blood flow thanks to the many exercises I had been doing before. They acknowledged that I was physically fit and healthy.

My heart attack was genetic. My father passed away from a heart attack. My mom and my younger brother also died of a heart attack. So, I inherited heart problems from my parents. However, one thing that took me to the verge of getting a heart attack was stress. I was taking too much stress in those days.

In the year 2009, I started my own brand. It was a small company. I aimed to get to 50 shops. So, I was heavily investing money to make more money. I was working hard, dealing with landlords, shopping centres issues, and other affairs. There was tremendous pressure on my shoulders. I had to employ people, train my daughter and son in law for the business, and carry the can as much as I could. At the same time, I was looking at everything from a savings point of view.

While my daughter and her husband were busy establishing the business in the south, they were constantly visiting sites, opening shops, overseeing the performance, and investing money. That, too, put immense pressure on my chest since I was the head of the empire. Apparently, I looked okay, but there was a lot of pressure on me. Handling a multi-million-pound business was no easy feat. You had to keep going on and on and never stop, no matter what.

After the operation, I was on rest for three months. My daughter and son-in-law were running the business all that time. When I recovered, I started going out. Slowly and gradually, I was back to the workout. Six months later, I was back to three miles running and three miles walking with some medication for a lifetime. I also started looking after the business right away. I couldn't let my business suffer, after all. I still had the end goal before my eyes; that is, I had to build the business and make it successful. However, the entire episode involving the heart attack changed my perspective on life.

Do you remember the chapter on my father's death and my life after that? I told you there that my life was so miserable after he died that I decided I would do all in my capacity to make money. I had only one goal in life – to make as much money as I could. This goal arose after my father's death and remained there until the time I got a heart attack some 30 odd years later.

I decided to work like a machine from the time I came to the UK. However, I was working so hard I didn't realise I was ruining my body. I was chasing the money day and night. I sometimes think if I had died that day, I would have left unfinished business for my family to sort out. It would have been an absolute nightmare for Mina, who didn't know how to run it. She was there with me, but she was not at the forefront of it. In my absence, other people could have tried to manipulate her in the wrong direction.

It was not just me who was shaken to the core; my family, too, was scared after this incident. It was super shocking for them since I wasn't ill. After I got normal, my family and I had a thoughtful conversation. My daughters and Mina told me that I needed to look after myself and slow down in the business a little. Our discussion made it clear to me that I was making a living but not making a living and that the latter was the most important thing in the world.

The best thing one can have during hard times is a loving, understanding, and supporting family by their side. I was lucky to have the same. My loving family told me to think about retirement to keep off work-related stress. They wanted me to relax and guide their kids through life by putting my experiences into their heads.

They assured me that they would be okay without me working around the clock. My daughters said, *"Dad, you have made enough money. Now, stop and relax. We are all educated enough that we can make a good living for ourselves. We need you alive and healthy"*. That provided me with a reason to go nice and slow in the business.

I realised that I could make less money but focus on surviving. I could not afford to do anything that would affect my health. So, slow and easy was the plan now. I knew that I needed to avoid taking the stress and look after my health. In this way, I could live long enough to spend quality time with my family and live the best life, which was something money couldn't buy me.

If you asked me, *"What's most important in life some 30 years ago?"* I would, without a second thought, have said, *"It's money"*. However, if you ask me the same question now, I would say, *"It's family"*. That's the change that happened after the heart attack, which was a wake-up call for me. It took me to go through a terrible heart attack to get my priorities right.

At the same time, I learned to be grateful for the things life had blessed me with. Thirty years ago, if I said I couldn't afford to stop, it would have much more sense. I would say I needed to keep going because back then, I had nothing in my name – no assets, no bank accounts, nothing. I just had a family to support. Now, on the other hand, I had built a business. I had assets to my name and enough money to enjoy my life in the best possible way. I had lived long enough to see my third generation.

I couldn't be more grateful for what life had given me. Perhaps if I kept on struggling, I would never get to enjoy the blessings I had received. Now, I focused on living my life, which meant spending quality time with my girls and their children. I now wanted to train my third generation for life ahead and make them smarter than my second generation.

Perhaps God had been sending signals my way for some years. Perhaps I caught one of the messages and decided to include Dimple and Vikesh into the business. When I was in the hospital, they ran the shops diligently. Now when I was going to withdraw from the business gradually, they had learned some of it. By the time I would retire, they would be on their own and need little help from me.

Chapter 23: Retirement

27th July 2011 is a date I can never forget. It's written in bold on the minds of my family and me. This was the day when I got my first ever heart attack and dozed off for about a week. On this day, I completed the family tradition of having a heart attack but luckily got to survive, unlike my parents and my brother, who breathed their last due to heart failure. Perhaps God had some solid plans for me. He wanted me to realise a number of things in time, and kudos to me for taking the lessons seriously.

When I recovered, I realised that my entire family had been in shock after seeing me on the bed, hanging between life and death. Mina had no clue how she would lead the family when I would be no more with them. We had so much work to do. My youngest daughter had yet to be married off. The business needed a supervisor who knew the ins and outs of it.

My daughters, on the other hand, were shaken by my illness. They looked forward to enjoying their lives with their family and having both their parents play a role in the upbringing of their children or future children. Every time they talked about coming to their parents' home, they wanted to see both their parents living their best life, smiling while chatting over, sipping a cup of coffee, playing with their grandchildren.

On my end, I wanted to spend lots of fun time with my wife and my girls. Throughout my career as a businessman, I barely went on carefree holidays or took my family out as often as I should. Now when I was on the bed, I realised how badly I needed to spend quality time with them. I wanted to enjoy our family life to the fullest before time ran out.

The months when I was in bed were a blessing in disguise. As much as I hated lying on bed and gazing at the walls, I was glad that I got enough time for some much-needed introspection. My wife and girls would look after me, help me walk to the bathroom, watch my diet, cook me healthy food, help me walk, and stay by me all the time. I loved waking up with them around and going to bed after bidding them a warm good night.

On one of the days when she was feeding me some piping hot soup, I took a closer look at Mina's hands. They were still beautiful, and the feeling of holding them wasn't much different from when we held each other for the first time on our wedding day. However, the veins of her hand showed how they have aged over time. *"How quickly time passed. We are entering old age. Have I done justice to my beloved wife for everything she has done for me?"* My thoughts went back to how I promised her a wonderful life *"someday"*. I felt I hadn't quite kept my promise, and time was running out.

Whenever I looked at Mina and how much she had sacrificed for me, I would think, *"One day, Mina and I will live our lives, and I'll travel with her to the best of places."* If you remember, we never went on a honeymoon because we had other priorities back then. Now, however, I had everything on my hands. The only thing I needed was a pause in work. Somewhere in my heart, I had decided that I would retire soon and give all my time to my family to fulfil the long due promise.

Before this tragedy struck us, we had no plans for retirement. I was planning to expand my business to the south and elsewhere. I dreamt of going all across the United Kingdom. The only things I would think about were planning, execution, and strategising for the business. Retirement was out of the question. I was fit and healthy, and so was my family. We never thought a time would come when we would have to think about winding up all of a sudden.

Thankfully, my eldest daughter, Dimple, and her husband were running parts of the business. So, I could sit back for some time and plan my future without having to rush back to the shops right after recovering from the heart attack. Dimple and Vikesh would visit us often and inquire about my health. We'd use this time to discuss some important work related things. I was glad that everything was going good in my absence.

I spent a lot of the time post heart attack asking some important 'what if' questions. Especially when I was alone, my thoughts would drift back to the same questions over and over again. They would ring loud in my ears, *"What if I didn't wake up that day?" "What would have become of my family in my absence?" "What if anybody tried to exploit them?"* And many more questions and scenarios would pop up in my head, and those made me restless.

Mina and I had worked hard been working hard for decades now. We always thought that we had a long road ahead, only we didn't know there was a terrible accident in the middle. Thank God this accident happened. Else, I'd be going on and on this road of life and reach the unseen end of the cliff and fall to the bottom.

I had been ill before, but every time I was unwell, I'd take a small break from work and bounce back in a few days time. This time, there was no bouncing back to normal. The queer thing about it was that there was nothing normal in life anymore. I worked on my health to get back on my feet, but that was not so I could get up from the bed and start running at the same pace in the same direction.

If I did that, I could see another heart attack in the next six months or one year. As I already explained in the last chapter, my physical body was not in bad shape. It was stress that was killing me, and genetics worsened the effects of stress on my body. I had always been a huge fan of adrenaline driven energy, but perhaps the extra dose of the same was proving detrimental to my body. It was time to put a lid on adrenaline reservoirs, or they'd come out in unnatural amounts and make me lose everything.

A voice came inside of me, *"Slow down, Shashi"*, and I took the message to heart. I thought I needed to keep my mind occupied, or I would go crazy. I had been using it so much for such a long time that it needed training for 'how to slow down without causing major damage to any other part of the body'. So, I decided to get back to work, but this time, I would be more conscious of my health and avoid all the negative stimuli that had the power to disrupt my normal body functioning.

Thoughts about selling the business were already there until my daughter and son in law joined it. That's when we started going harder and faster in expansion, and then selling it took a backseat. It took me a brutal heart attack to revert to my original plan. *"Start looking for potential buyers, Shashi"* was the latest resolve now.

The thing was, we had to keep the business going in full swing if we wanted to sell it. Anybody interested in buying our business would have a close look at the accounts, the performance of each individual shop, the details of the suppliers and employees, etc. We would get a good bid if we kept all parts of the business running just perfectly. Hence, I jumped back into action and started looking out for potential buyers in the meantime.

I spread the word among my networks and people I interacted with that we were considering prospects, and leads started pouring in. We did manage to bump into some potential candidates after some time hunting for them. I received a couple of calls from people who were interested in buying our business and got some reasonable rates. I knew, "It's time to take the issue to Mina, Dimple, and Vikesh". Next, all three of us sat down in the drawing-room of our home and discussed the idea at length.

We discussed my ailing health and how things were going to be when I couldn't afford to give a lot of time to the business. My kids knew how important it was for me to retire, and they agreed to the plan. Once that was done, the timing of this step came under discussion. All three of us had our own perspectives. Towards the end of the discussion, however, we decided to let the Olympics pass, and then we'd proceed with the selling.

Fast forward to the Olympic season; we had a great time. Our sales skyrocketed thanks to the location of some of our stores. The general public and tourists went crazy for the coffee, and we were everywhere. The amazing response of this season had us stall the selling for the time being and keep going. A lot of other entities appreciated our work, and due to some other reasons, we had to put the idea of selling our business on the side.

For the next five years, we continued with expansion. Now we had almost twenty-five shops running under our brand name. It was an amazing journey. Fortunately, I got to lead the business without falling terribly ill and was more than happy to have seen my business reach the pinnacle in my lifetime. I was looking after myself more and was conscious not to take too much pressure about anything.

In the year 2018, the realisation that I had been working like a mule all through the day hit me again, and I decided to sell the business once and for all. This was the end of over twenty years of working around the clock. We had given our heart and soul to it, and now we sold it to someone who could take the venture to the next level. As for myself, I was ready to utilise whatever time I had in the best way by looking after my family.

Right after retirement, we planned our extensive vacations. We had had vacations before, but I wanted to travel around the world free of all sorts of care. Here was my dream coming true. We went to some of the most exotic places around the globe. We even visited our homeland India and met our relatives there. I took Mina to her village to meet her siblings and relatives.

We saw the famous Taj Mehal in India and even walked by the beeches of Hawaii. I took Mina's hand, and together we walked on the sand with the enormous waves touching our feet as they declined near the shore. Our gait reminded us of the time when we took the *pheray* around the fire (*agni*) that made us man and wife. In all those years, we had changed a lot from the outside, but deep inside our hearts, our love and commitment towards each other had only intensified.

We smiled like news weds as we supported one another balance through the powerful currents that came occasionally. Those were some of the best moments of our lives. Never had I ever thought that I would be having such a beautiful time with the love of my life with zero thoughts about the business surging up every now and then. Life seemed perfect when we were free and together.

Now that when I look back at my decision of selling the business, I pat myself on the back. If let's assume I still had it, I would be worrying myself sick. Due to covid, all the business and even entire economies of the nations suffered badly. All the food chains experienced closures. Thankfully, I was spared the sitting at home and waiting for the shops to open, which was inevitable due to covid. Now, I sit at home and spend some love filled moments with my wife and play with my grandchildren. That gives me such enormous pleasure that I wouldn't trade it for anything in the world.

If you ask me what's the biggest negative thing about retirement, I would say it's not earning money. You have to use the money you have already earned, and that would deplete slowly and gradually. I would not say I don't miss carrying out business. There are times when I look at the opportunities and go, *"Here's a great one. Let's, oh, but I have retired"*. In those moments, I sit back and enjoy retirement. I may convey them to others who I see potential in. To this day, aspiring businesspersons or those already in the business approach me for seeking advice, and I feel proud in helping them.

People tell you that you are your own boss when you have a business. Well, that is true to some extent. However, I experienced the real taste of being a boss when I retired. I can spend my time the way I want to. I can go anywhere I want. I don't have to take permission from anybody or have to worry about some unfinished business. I have plenty of time on my hands, and that's what I call freedom.

Now, I have enough savings to afford us a comfortable life after retirement, and I have enough time to give to my family. Mina and I are reliving our childhood with our grandkids. My daughters and their children come over quite often. We recollect old memories when we get together. Oftentimes, we end up planning a trip to some new place. I cannot help thanking God for granting me everything I asked for, from a successful multi-million pounds business to a loving family.

Here's a picture of us post-retirement.

Chapter 24: Legacy

I had always abhorred our financial position in society back in Kaliari. The feeling stayed the same when we came to the UK. In fact, the only motivation I had in a significant part of my life was to break the cycle of poverty and make lots of money. Then, I did not quite understand that being born into poverty was no less than a blessing. Had I not seen the lack of money, I would not have come this far chasing it. The lack of money created an urge in me to acquire it all the more desperately.

Every individual or entity leaves behind them a legacy for the people to come. When I think about it and analyse the life of my father, I can tell he left a brilliant legacy for me. From a very young age, I had seen him working harder and harder to make both ends meet. His goals may not be very grand, the ways he met them deserved huge applause.

My father never missed a day at work. He would always be up and doing the business, which was farming for him. On the character side, he was supremely honest, trustworthy and truthful. I never saw him taking advantage of anyone, even when he could have done that during his time as the village surpunj. The examples of justice that he set through his decisions motivated us to follow the same path in our lives.

My father left exceptional traits and habits as a legacy for all his children. We had a perfect example of him before us. Now when I look back at my life in retrospection, I can see where I got some of my best traits from. Dad didn't leave us any wealth or property, but he gave us some highly-priced characteristics which people run after all their lives and fail to acquire.

When they ask me, *"How could you work so hard, Shashi?"* I can tell them, *"I'm a proud farmer's son. Working hard comes naturally to me"*. I had never seen my parents shy away from work, and so I never shirked work either. I hope my next generation and those that come after that continue the legacy and benefit from the life and experiences of their ancestors.

In the last chapters, I discussed with you how I try to be active in upbringing my grandchildren. The fact is my daughters wanted me to be their mentor. They had seen me starting out with very little and building an empire step by step through courage, determination and perseverance, and they want me to instil the same qualities into their kids. The problem with my third generation is that they are born in a time when they have everything at their disposal. They haven't tasted rejection, failure, and being broke, which are the best teachers in life. Hence, to familiarise themselves with life as it is, they need the guidance of somebody who has seen all of that.

I have always taught my children to keep going all the time and give no excuses. Life is full of ups and downs. My business journey was also a bumpy ride, but I did not quit. I would always be there at work, no matter what. If something didn't go in my favour, I was quick to modify it instead of avoiding it. You make mistakes; you get hurt, but you should always come up with a better strategy and a better approach.

I have emphasised this in the previous chapters, and I am saying this here again. Hard work does not kill anyone, and there is no shortcut to hard work. When you are at a stage where you don't know how things work, you have two options. One, you can learn the job fifty per cent and count on others, your employees, partners, or even God, to make it work for you. Two, you can give your one hundred per cent, learn all about your work and kill it without having to rely on the others so much.

I always advise my children to choose the second option, and they have done that in their careers. When young, my daughters would study hard and not leave anything on chance. That way, they would always ace their exams and end up clearing some of the toughest ones. Now, they are working in the top corporations in important positions. You see, the top companies value the employees who know their work.

To gain knowledge of anything, you have to work hard at it. This applies more to people who are not in an excellent position in a career, job, or business. They will have to work hard, especially in the early stages, to gain expertise in their respective field. When I started out, I barely knew anything about running a coffee shop, and I was aware of that. So, I went as far as Australia to see their functioning and visited multiple shops to learn the basics. Then when I finally started, I made sure to remain available from early morning to night so that I could learn all the aspects of the business.

A lot of people make the mistake of doing smart work when what they actually need is hard work. I always told my girls, *"When you're learning something for the first time, put in as much hard work as you could. Then, when you know the ins and outs of it, work smarter"*. That lesson I learnt from my business. If I had put in smart work earlier and got the employees to do the job while I only supervised, they could have easily dodged me. Or, when a problem arose, I wouldn't know how to deal with it. I'd be counting on the people running it. In other words, the staff that knew the work would be running the business and not me.

Another thing I teach my grandkids is to never run from challenges. They are a part of life and will keep coming till we leave the planet. Hence, it's pointless evading them. The best thing is to take them by the horns. This way, you will never be afraid of them. Rather you'd look forward to them because every challenge leaves you stronger and better.

In business, I would try to predict the problems that could come our way and find solutions beforehand. They never scared me. Also, I inherited the problem-solving approach from my parents, and I want to transfer the same approach to the next generations. I had seen my father probing the farm-related issues and finding the best solutions to them. Whenever something was wrong with the crops, my father would examine them and find ways to fix them. That is what I did too in business, and I can vouch that it always saves you.

We are surrounded by competition everywhere. You enter a career, and you'll feel as if the entire world is in the same career as yours, thanks to soaring competition in all walks of life. In business, too, the markets are competitive. You may be the pioneer in something, but other people will crowd it very soon. There was a time when McDonald's was one of a kind, and in a short period of time, we got fast food companies selling their varieties of burgers and fries all around us.

What I mean to say is that we live in a competitive world. We'll always have competitors. We cannot keep them from entering the game. At best, we can stay ahead of the game so that our name goes out to people's ears and they know who to come to for a cup of coffee, for instance. While running the coffee business, I needed to be aware of all the ways we could entice the customers to buy from us.

A good product is not enough. You need people to know you exist, so you market your product using the most commonly used platforms. Then you see others putting out special deals, and you have to follow suit. Likewise, we had to see what was 'in' those days. If there was a trend of giving special offers or discounts to regular customers, we had to add it in our services too. So, there was always so much going on in the market that required me to stay updated with all the changes if I were to survive. Had I continued in a conventional way, nobody would have known that Love Coffee existed.

In such a competitive environment, you cannot afford to lose your focus at any time. You have to stay vigilant and receptive to all the trends around you. That is exactly what I educate my daughters, not necessarily regarding business, but about life in general. They should always know what's happening around them and keep an eye on the clues regarding the future.

I want my girls to be ready to face whatever comes their way, and that is the key to leading a meaningful life. They never take no for an answer like their dad, who got this from his dad. Problems sometimes seem bigger than our mental capacity, but there is always a way out. When our mind is occupied with negative emotions of all sorts, such as anxiety, fear, and hopelessness, we would have a hard time getting to the solution. It is only when we push such sentiments to the back that we can really focus on the solutions.

Usually, the solutions are right there before our eyes, and we act blind to them. To succeed in finding them or creating them, if the need arises, you have to develop a solution-oriented approach. I can tell from experience that it is the best approach and teach my kids and their kids to adopt it for life.

Another thing I teach them is to never miss the opportunity when it knocks on their door. It does not happen very often that opportunities come your way. They are always in high demand. If you don't grab them, somebody else will, leaving you with regrets. So, never give reasons for missing opportunities. If you aren't ready when you see the opportunity, prepare yourself and get ready, but don't lose the opportunity. It might not come twice.

Remember when my brother and I were running the franchise together, and we didn't buy an excellent site we came across for our shop and the guy who bought it was doing crazy numbers? That's what I mean by missing the opportunity. One of the reasons I parted ways with my brother was that he was not quick in grabbing opportunities. I knew if I stayed with him, I'd be regretting many more decisions. So, I went separately to do things my way while, of course, maintaining a cordial relationship on the personal level.

Almost everything I know today I have learned it the hard way. No university could have taught me what my father and my circumstances have taught me. I learned most of the things through practical experience and exposure to the real world. My daughters are in a much better position than I ever was. They have the option to quit their job if they want or start a new career afresh if they like. They have me to guide them in business if they want to start one. They also have my friends and networks to benefit from.

On the other hand, since they have seen their father's struggles and hardships, they understand the value of time, money and prestige. They know these things are never offered on a platter. You have to earn them. As long as I am here, I'll keep reminding them of important lessons of my life so that they know real stuff.

When I look at my grandchildren, however, I am not sure how they will turn out to be. They are better off than I was in every way. So, they might not know how this world works, how they should think, what they should do, to what extent they should do that to be ahead of whatever game they're in.

The next generation is usually more robust and successful than the previous one, and that is how it should be. It will make me the happiest if my grandkids are a thousand times better than their grandfather. However, they don't have hardships of the kind I faced to teach them some real lessons. That is why I'm writing this book for them to read one day and live my life and get essential takeaways from it.

My grandkids are small now. I don't know if I'd live long enough to be with them through their youth or so. Hence this book is an attempt to familiarise them with my life when I am not there anymore. I can give them lessons after lessons, but it would not help. When my grandchildren read this book, they would get those lessons in a far more effective way than me teaching them like a school teacher.

267

I wish one day, my grandkids read my book and say, *"Grandpa was a wonderful man. We'll be like him and do even better"*. When I see my family, I feel super proud of leaving a positive legacy behind. My girls are immensely happy and proud of what I have achieved coming from a small place in India. They are putting in their children's life what I put into their life, and that gives me a reason always to be happy.

I have always had high regard for people who lead by example, and I am delighted to be on the list of those today. When I talk to my kids or their kids, I don't say whatever comes to my mind. I speak from experience, rather vast experience. I want my next generations to walk the same path and set an example for their following generations.

Chapter 25: Today And Tomorrow

When I was a young boy, I used to think one hundred rupees was a lot of money. It translates into roughly one pound. Today, I see my younger grandkids talking in terms of millions and multi-millions, and I see how much more knowledgeable and advanced my new generation is than I was. They know the value of money so well and know how much is a lot and how much is little. It just amazes me how the three generations of our family are so dramatically different from one another.

Today, when I see my family doing great and the people of my village only a little better than when I was there, I feel like giving a big pat on my back and say, "You made the right decision, Shashi". The images of Kaliari never feel old when I think of them. The place looks so fresh, so alive to me even today. I still go there and feel the antiquity of my village. Even though it has improved with time, but the rigid norms and traditions are still alive. It's hard for me to realise how substantially my life has transformed.

When I came into the UK, I had nothing in my pocket. The only treasure I had were my mother, my brother, and many big dreams. My brother was the support system I had. He financed us in the beginning, and he was the one who sponsored us here. My mother was everything for me. She was the source of guidance and blessings and was my biggest well-wisher. These two important people offered all kinds of support I needed to settle in a new place and start a new chapter of life.

I had a powerful motivation to make money in bulk, and I was willing to give everything it took. I had already experienced the world at its most brutal, and I knew the only way to earn respect in society's eyes was to get rich. Hence, I took admission in a language centre where I took foundational English classes for some months and jumped into the market to start making money straight away. Throughout the early stages and the upcoming ones, my dreams pushed me to keep going and never look back.

I was both smart and naive at the beginning of my practical life. For instance, I knew how to talk to people, convince them, make a deal, and be good at whatever I did. However, since I was young, there were many situations I encountered for the first time in my life. I was naïve, and through experience, I got to the part where I learned about the taxes, laws, and mistakes that could land me into trouble, for instance, as well as the things that could boost my sales.

Time is the best teacher. You can always count on it to make you a better version of yourself, provided you are willing to take on new challenges. It's like entering a tunnel in small size and becoming ten times bigger while exiting it. I took on bigger challenges and therefore grew faster. It was not easy for a person who could not speak a word of English to run a successful business and retire as a multi-millionaire.

I can vouch for one thing. Life trains you in the best possible ways. You have to be ready for all those capacity building exercises and have the desire to achieve your goals, and you will find yourself there very soon. If you are not good enough, keep working on yourself to be worthy of the position you aim at, and you will get there. Then, set the next target and keep adjusting yourself to the requirements of the new place. Rest assured that when you have done that, you will get what you have been dreaming of.

Your intention in whatever you do is vital. When you know you are doing right and you are optimistic about making an impact on somebody's life, you get through all sorts of difficulties and achieve your objectives. Since my intention was always good, I had lots of people to motivate me, and I never felt like giving up. I knew I had to make my family strong and provide them with everything they needed to live an upgraded life, and that kept me going hard.

Now that I look back, I believe my impoverished family background and bitter experiences with people turned out in my favour, or rather I made them my motivation for doing great. I had experienced so much agony that I was bent on working hard and making money so that I could give the best life to my children and earn respect in people's eyes. Thus, I had ample sources of motivation both inside and in my external environment.

I feel proud of myself for achieving whatever I have achieved in life, keeping in mind where I came from. From learning basic English to finalising deals with big businessmen, I have come a long way. Now, I look forward to inspiring others to start their journey or go stronger if they're already in the process and make big numbers.

The purpose of putting my life story and narrating my struggles before you is to let you know that you can control your fate and take many decisions in your hand. No matter where you stand in life at this point, there are always prospects for doing better tomorrow. Life does not offer you anything on a platter. You will have to earn everything you want, be it money, love or respect, through hard work, commitment, and discipline. You may be standing at zero level at this point, but know that you'll have to improve one notch, then another and another and that is how you get to the top.

Now when I look at my kids, I feel contented to have built a strong foundation for them. It works like the construction industry. You want to erect high rise buildings; you have to do strong groundwork. I wanted my children and their children to do exceptionally well in their lives, so I improved myself in terms of knowledge, expertise, exposure, skills, and personality traits. I see my efforts bearing fruits when my kids and grandkids perform better than I did in various aspects of life.

When I started out, the only goal I had in mind was working hard and making money and working harder and making more money. Then Mina came, and we both worked together. Time passed, and we grew into a family of six, including my mother and three girls. I kept achieving one target after another, with each phase ending into a newer set of targets. We went from running a convenience store to coffee shops and multiplying them through the years.

Business had its share of hardships and bad times. There were times when we had to take tough decisions, but we did it successfully. Being an entrepreneur, I loved the adrenaline surges I used to have back in the days when my shops were up and running. I am delighted to have had such a rich experience in the business world. In those years, I learned more than any school could have taught me. I still feel blessed to have acquired uncountable skills and traits from the business world.

I may not be working today, but people from different places come to me to seek guidance on business. They approach me to help them with decision-making, planning, strategy formulation, boosting sales, building clientele, and so many other things. I take so much pride in being helpful to aspiring or struggling businesspersons. It amazes some people how a high school graduate could possess such an astute mind and know so much.

I tell people I learned from the best teacher in the world, that is, time. I also tell people I learned business the best way, that is, by observing how it's done and practising it every single day. I would make mistakes and derive a lesson from them for the next time. When I was learning the tricks of the trade, my young family was growing fast. They were acing at school and doing great in all aspects of life.

When my girls grew up, and Mina and I were nearing old age, we became more closely knit than ever. Heart attack taught me what the most important entity in life was. Now, I am glad that together, Mina and I have raised a lovely family. We taught our girls the best of values and made them highly productive individuals. All three of our girls are highly educated, and they have worked in the corporate sector in excellent positions. They are confident, self-assured and ambitious women. I love seeing them acing at their jobs or raising their kids.

Having retired from business, I sometimes miss those days when my schedule was packed and I was wholly occupied with work. After all, I am an entrepreneur. However, I don't waste my today thinking about yesterday. I think in terms of future. I still look at business prospects and make mental calculations when I bump into an opportunity because it thrills me. I still love discussing business with my friends and acquaintances and offer my counselling to those I see spot passion for business in.

My today is different from, rather better than, my yesterday in many ways. I feel I'm spending my time in the best way possible. I can now talk to Mina for hours and hours without getting tired. Mina and I play with our grandkids, ask them questions, answer their queries, and have lots of fun time together. On some days, our girls come over, and we laugh our heads off, reminiscing old memories.

Attending to the next generation is one of the best things I do. It's like raising my girls one more time, perhaps even better. I missed a lot of phases of my daughters' lives thanks to my busy schedule at work, but life allowed me to witness my grandkids growing up. There are times when Mina and I become kids with our grandchildren, and that is a blessing not many people get.

It's not that my grandchildren are not very smart. They are ten times clever than my daughters were at their age. Mina and I witness their feats of intelligence every single day, and we cannot help grasping, "We were so stupid at this age, no?" They make us realise that our family tree is blossoming and that is one of the best feelings in the whole wide world.

Our grandkids win the same accolades my daughters used to win at their schools. So, they are continuing the legacy and doing even better, I would say. They are inquisitive. They are smart and ambitious. They are calculative. They had more facilities than my kids growing up and, therefore, fare better than their parents in everything.

When I think of it now, I see how much power money has. It does not only increase your purchasing power; it elevates the lifestyle of your generations. Had I been only a little better than my parents, my children would not have studied from top universities of the world, and their children would not have been this smart and qualified had they not received the education and environment they now have.

That is not to say that the future of the upcoming generation is always reliant on the previous one. You can always take the steering in your hand and take the route you want to. You can take that jump up the ladder provided you do what is required of you. I have presented my example before you so that I may be able to motivate you to whatever extent I can to take up the challenge and play the big game.

The purpose of this book was to help people turn their lives around just as I did and to show it is very much possible. I would be content if this book could help aspiring entrepreneurs get started on their journey and make their lives better.

To all such people, I have left several tips and messages throughout this book. Here is a summary of it. Work hard, work smart, think positive, have the will to do good in life, and never give up. Don't just get started. Know what you are doing and where you want to see yourself in the next couple of years. In other words, have a map of your life in mind, set up a path, follow the track, hit goalposts one by one, keep deadlines for every five or six years and meet them with courage and determination. Follow these tips, and nothing will stop you from achieving big in life.

Once you have achieved a milestone, try giving back to society. That can take any form. You can give away money, knowledge, or even help someone by guiding them to the right path. That way, you will always feel you're doing something meaningful in life and won't feel empty from inside. I spend a lot of time doing charity these days and helping people out in business, and I can tell it gives you the happiness nothing else can.

Life blessed me with everything I wanted – money, knowledge, networks, friends, family and time. I can't be more grateful for all those blessings. Out of all these things, those I enjoy the most are family, time and, of course, a cup of nice warm coffee.

Printed in Great Britain
by Amazon

83216476R00163